THE LONDON MILK TRAIL

The London Milk Trail

Megan Hayes

Dedicated to my parents,
Dan and Eliza Jane Lloyd,
and all who followed the milk trail

First published in: 2015

Published with the financial support
of the Welsh Books Council

ISBN: 978-1-84527-551-8

Cover design: Eleri Owen

Published by Gwasg Carreg Gwalch,
12 Iard yr Orsaf, Llanrwst, Wales LL26 0EH
tel: 01492 642031
fax: 01492 641502
email: books@carreg-gwalch.com
website: www.carreg-gwalch.com

Contents

I. YMADAEL

'Roedd crafanc y nawdegau
Yn turio at fêr y tir;
Eidionnau'n mynd am ganu
Cyn brigo o flewyn ir,
A chorddi'r 'menyn cymell
Ar feddal hafddydd hir.

Fe droes Dai bach, bentymor
I'r stryd o'r crinllyd lain,
Gan gamu'n esgus-dalog
Dros riniog bwth ei nain,
Yn llanc â da ei logell
Ond sofren felen, fain.

II. DYCHWELYD

Hanner canrif ym mwrllwch Soho,
A chloes y siop am yr olaf dro;
Dringodd binaclau ei alltud werin -
Plas yn y faesdref a blaensedd yn Jewin.

Yng ngwydd y dyrnaid o hynafgwyr syn,
Yn eu brethyn du a'u coleri gwyn,
Rhyw uchel Fehefin, drwy bersawr gwair hadau
Aed â Dai'r gwas bach yn ôl at ei dadau.

John Roderick Rees
Cerddi John Roderick Rees

Foreword

This remarkable story of enterprising Welsh dairymen and women in London should be seen in the wider context of life in one of the world's greatest cities.

The Welsh have been a noticeable presence in London since the days of Henry Tudor. His quarter-Welsh extraction was more than enough to endear him to the disoriented people of fifteenth-century Wales. The army of soldiers, workers and court officials who came to London in 1485 with their new monarch, Henry VII, included a fair number of Welsh.

This was, in effect, the birth of the 'London Welsh', an ethnic community whose shape and character have changed a great deal over the past six centuries. This was a community which arguably reached its zenith in late Victorian and Edwardian times, an age of grand Nonconformist chapels and other impressive city-wide networks.

This was the world inhabited by the Welsh dairy families of London, most of which had roots in the villages and small towns of Cardiganshire. Theirs is a tale of exceptionally hard work, modest lifestyles, and innovative businesses. They gambled everything on a risky journey from Tregaron, Pennant, Bwlch-llan, Bronant, Bethania, Llanon, and so many other impoverished places, to build new life in London.

Many succeeded beyond their wildest dreams. Others failed, and paid a brutal price.

This is a story that sheds new light not only on the London Welsh, but also on the people of Ceredigion.

Megan Hayes is to be warmly congratulated on her achievement.

Huw Edwards

Introduction

Migration is a familiar concept. It describes how individuals and families leave their native countries for a variety of reasons, generally economic or religious, in search of a better life.

This book relates the migration of people, in the main from Cardiganshire, to the milk trade in London, in search of a better life than that available in their homeland.

It was a search for a life that would lift them from the poverty and lack of employment opportunities in the home country, especially so in Cardiganshire and North Carmarthenshire

The movement could be said to be a development from the tradition of droving. From this came cow keeping in the metropolis in order to supply the growing demand for milk with its short shelf life. Eventually, dairies, retailing milk and other dairy goods became well established and firmly in the hands of emigres from this part of Wales.

It is a story well rooted in the memories of people from these counties but rapidly disappearing into myth and worse, misconception. This book does not aim to be an academic treatment of the topic though such sources have been well drawn on in the early chapters. Rather, the aim is to capture the story of the lives, difficulties and expectations of those who made the transition.

It is hoped that it is not too late to capture and relate the experiences of those who left to seek a better life in a 'far country' and it is in this spirit that this volume is offered.

A two pound note issued by Banc y Ddafad Ddu – one of the Drover Banks

The Drovers

The droving of cattle from Wales to London is long established as part of the history of milk marketing in the English capital. As the historian R. J. Colyer shows in several articles and books, there is evidence that the cattle trade has existed since the middle of the thirteenth century. However, one can consider those who started their journey in Cardiganshire as something far more than forerunners or establishers of the London Welsh milk market.

On examining the history of droving in the nineteenth century, one is aware of not only the drovers' marketing skills but of their many other attributes. Not only were they entrepreneurs but they also enjoyed wider interests. Some established schools, whilst others became ministers or composers of hymns which are today very much a part of the Welsh religious voice. Some were responsible for setting up the first local banks later taken over by national businesses.

There is much more to the story of the drovers than simply driving cattle from Wales to England. The Welsh always had cattle to export. The climatic and terrain conditions prevailing in West Wales were responsible for establishing cattle rearing as one of the earliest main occupations. By the middle of the nineteenth century driving cattle to London on foot to be sold, was an important trade. It is estimated that over the years some 300,000 beasts from Wales to southern England, including London. As well as cattle, sheep, pigs, horses, geese and turkeys were driven along this long and hazardous journey. But here, as the milk trade is our concern, we will concentrate on cattle alone.

Cattle fairs were held in various centres throughout Wales. In Cardiganshire, the main marketplaces were numerous and included Tregaron and Cardigan and across the border in Cilgerran and Eglwyswrw. These were convenient places for farmers to sell their spare cattle to dealers. The bargaining entailed lengthy haggling until the deal was settled by striking palms of hands.

E. O. James, in an article in the first issue of *The Carmarthen Historian* on the county's drovers quotes from the poem by D.E. Davies of Llan-y-crwys, seen in its entirety in Appendix 1:

O ffeiriau Sir Benfro, da mawrion i gyd,
A'u cyrnau gan mwyaf yn llathen o hyd,
O Hwlffordd, Treletert a Narberth rhai braf,
O Grymych, Maenclochog a Thŷ-gwyn ar Daf.

O Lanarth, o Lanbed, Ffair Rhos a Thalsarn,
O Ledrod, Llanddalis y delent yn garn;
O ffeiriau Llanbydder, Penuwch a Chross Inn,
Da duon, da gleision ac ambell un gwyn.

O ffeiriau Caerfyrddin, da perton ac ir,
Ac ambell fyswynog o waelod y sir.
Doi da Castellnewydd a Chynwil i'r lan
At dda Dyffryn Tywi, i gyd i'r un man.

From the Pembrokeshire fairs, cows all fat and gross,
Their horns mostly measured a full yard across,
From Narberth, Letterstone and Haverfordwest,
From Crymych, Maenclochog and Whitland, the best.

From Llanarth and Lampeter, Talsarn and Ffair Rhos,
From Lledrod, Llanddalis, in rows upon rows,
Llanybydder, Penuwch and Cross Inn, what a sight
Some blacks and some blues, and one or two whites.

From the fairs of Carmarthen, fine cows in a flow,
And one or two barrens from further below,
From Newcastle Emlyn and Cynwil, in throng,
To the Vale of the Tywi, they all came along.

The cattle that were sold would be herded and collected in various centres to prepare for the journey. Tregaron was the centre always used by the West Wales drovers as it was the last low-lying centre on the journey from Wales. Before setting out, the chief drover would ensure that every animal had been shod. The Tregaron drovers had their own smiths. The shoes were made from small pieces of metal and each piece firmly fixed on every hoof using three nails; the metal was smeared with butter to prevent rust. For a long journey, such as the one to London, the cattle would be shod front and rear; for shorter journeys, only the front hooves were shod. One of the key members of the team was the man responsible for felling the animal about to be shod. Shoeing was a difficult task, as described by R. T. Jenkins in his book *Y Ffordd yng Nghymru* (The Road in Wales)

A rope was tied around the cow's leg and tightened, causing the animal to topple. Its head was kept down, causing it to drop on its head. Then the feet were tied together and a stick placed between them to ensure solidity. Following the throwing and the tying, the smith – or two smiths – would quickly fix the shoes.

E. O. James quotes another poem that describes the work in detail. The unnamed poet could well be E. D. Davies again:

Yn y ffair fe welaf dyrfa
O fystechi mewn cae porfa
Ger Pont Twrch, ac i'w pedoli

At y gwaith fe eir o ddifri
Deio Hendy Cwrdd 'Sgerdawe
Ydyw'r cyntaf un i ddechre.
Cydio wna yng nghorn y bustach.
A rhed ganddo gamymhellach.
Fe rydd dro i'r corn yn sydyn
A'r anifail syrth fel plentyn.
Gyda rhaff daw eraill ato
I glymu'r pedair coes rhag cicio.
Nawr mae off, y gof a'r offer
Yn pedoli ar ei gyfer
A chyn hir, y bustach ola
Sydd â'i bedol yn y borfa.

After the fair I see a host
Of steers in a grassy field
Near Twrch Bridge to be shod,
A task undertaken with much purpose.
The first to set about the task
Is Deio from Chapel House, Esgairdawe,
He first grabs the creature's horn
And runs with it a further yard;
Suddenly, the horn he twists
And the creature drops like a child.
Others arrive with a rope
To tie the legs to stop them kicking.
And now it's all go, the smith with tackle
Speedily secures the shoes,
And very soon the final steer
Has its shoes among the grass.

In Tregaron the cattle were herded below Pen Pica, a hill
behind the taverns of the Talbot and the Bush next door.
They were then driven across Tŷ Gwyn fields towards Cwm

Berwyn; this would be used as an overnight station by Dafydd Isaac, a prominent drover in his day. The cattle would then be driven at a pace of some two miles an hour covering between fifteen and twenty miles a day. The drovers' pay varied between one shilling and three shillings a day with a bonus at the journey's end. To enhance their earnings, they sold milk along the way.

It was from the uplands of Cwm Berwyn that another drover, Jenkin Williams, Derigaron was inspired to write a verse that was not wholly complimentary to Tregaron:

> *Mae Tregaron fach yn mwgi.*
> *Nid oes fater tai hi'n llwgu;*
> *Os bydd newydd drwg ar gered,*
> *Yn Nhregaron cewch ei glywed.*

> Dear Tregaron town is smoking
> It matters not should it be starving,
> Should there be any bad news around,
> It's in Tregaron it will be found.

Tregaron was a centre of importance as it was sited at the southern end of the Abergwesyn pass. The road was known as the Drovers' Road and the big advantage was that it was not a toll road. Avoiding turnpike roads and their attendant toll gates was important because it could cost up to a shilling a head to take cattle through these gates. This, of course, was per journey, and not the toll for every individual gate. Even then, a shilling a head was a considerable sum when a herd could consist of hundreds of animals.

The head drover ensured that the drovers were adequately clad. Their outfits were described to Richard Colyer by Professor E. G. Bowen, an authority on the social history of Cardiganshire. They were attired in farm servants' smocks and wore long woollen stockings and strong leggings of Bristol Brown Paper. They wore wide brimmed hats to protect themselves from the seasonal elements. Every drover carried soap and brown paper; the soap was rubbed into the woollen stockings as waterproofing and the brown paper served as a water-repellent vest when they slept outdoors. Only the head drover slept indoors.

The road from Tregaron led up towards Abergwesyn, Cwmdulas, Newbridge on Wye, Radnor and Kington and onwards across the border as far as Leominster. At Southam the drovers chose Northampton or turned southwards towards London, and particularly Barnet.

The herds varied in size between two and three hundred head of cattle. Similarly the number of drovers varied according to the number of cattle. Rhys Morgan from Tregaron, known as the King of Northampton employed twelve drovers to herd three hundred cattle. One of five drover brothers, he was regarded as a head drover; he continued droving until the beginning of the last century and according to Evan Jones in his book *Cerdded Hen Ffeiriau* (Following Old Fairs) he was the first to use cheques.

There were shoeing centres, or smithies along the way as well as taverns providing sustenance for the drovers and lodgings for the head drover. The location of such a tavern was marked by three Scotch Pines growing outside. In England, three yew trees were more usual. These were symbols that drovers were welcome for the night rather than indications of tavern sites. Whilst the head drover slept indoors, the others slept in nearby fields. Frequently, the younger ones slept with the cattle in order to be close enough to attend to them during the night. Lying in such close proximity to the cattle was also a means of keeping warm.

STORE   TILL OP NO. TRANS. DATE
0628   1 781165 104116 23/08/2015 15:21

VAT Reg No. GB 108 2770 24

App Seq: 02
AID: A000000003010
Ref: 0000001261?
Auth Code: 621506
For your Records
Please Keep This Receipt

PIN VERIFIED

TOTAL   GBP55.00
AMOUNT   GBP55.00
Please debit my account

ICC   CP SALE

Visa Credit
****************5973

23/08/2015 15:20:19
M:***68372
P:W3433095   T:1****1029

*** CARDHOLDER COPY ***
- - - - - - - - - - - - - - - -
Apply now at thewaterstonescard.com
ON ITEMS WORTH £55.00
EARNED YOU 165 POINTS TODAY
THE WATERSTONES CARD WOULD HAVE
THE WATERSTONES CARD

Visa   £55.00

£55.00

Balance to pay
No. items 3

Money Off   **-£4.00**
9781847921208
RAJ AT WAR, THE   £25.00
9781846144387
FALL OF THE OTTOMAN   £25.00
9781845275518
LONDON MILK TRAIL,   £9.00

SALE TRANSACTION

01267 233330
SA31 1PR
Carmarthen
14-15 Gu...

rights.

Waterstones

Refunds & exchanges

Waterstones

Refunds & exchanges

Again, according to Richard Colyer, the price of lodging remained constant throughout the century, at a groat, or four pence per head in summer, and six pence in the winter.

Tregaron's head drover would normally stay in Shepherds Bush, and that for three pence a night with an additional three pence for breakfast. Shepherds Bush, west of London, had common land where cattle and other animals were put to pasture before being driven on to Smithfield.

The majority of the cattle were Welsh Blacks of around three years of age. They were known as Welsh Runts, were of the same size as Belted Galloways and they could survive on poor grazing and in cold, wet weather. E.O. James in *The Carmarthen Historian* of 1961 also includes other breeds. He has good reason to believe that the herds were reinforced with breeds such as the Castlemartin and the Brecon Border White-headed Cattle, the precursors of the Hereford Cattle. According to some historians, among them Cledwyn Fychan of Llanddeiniol, these were semi wild cows like the old 'Da Gleision Glanteifi', (The Teifiside Blues), also known as 'The Old Breed', descendants of the original Strata Florida Abbey cattle. They were very productive milkers and buyers from London would travel to Cardiganshire to purchase them.

The drovers were regarded by town dwellers with some suspicion and even trepidation. In *The Farmers Magazine* of 1856, there is an interesting account if rather prejudiced of the drovers seen in Barnet Fair.

Imagine some hundreds of bullocks like an immense forest of horns, propelled hurriedly towards you amid the hideous and uproarious shouting of a set of semi-barbarous drovers who value a restive bullock far beyond the life of a human being, driving their mad and noisy herds over every person they meet if not fortunate enough to get out of their way; closely followed by a drove of unbroken wild Welsh ponies, fresh from their native hills all of them loose and unrestrained as the oxen that preceded them; kicking, rearing and biting each other amid the unintelligible anathemas of their human attendants ... the noisy 'hurrahs' of lots of 'un-English speaking' Welshmen who may have just sold some of their native bovine stock whilst they are to be seen throwing up their long-worn, shapeless hats high in the air, as a type of Taffy's delight, uttering at the same time a trade (*sic*) of gibberish which no-one can understand but themselves.

It must be that this was the kind of scene that led to the founding of the Welsh Calvinistic Methodist Chapel in Cock Lane, Smithfield in 1774, the first Welsh house of worship to be established in London. This was just one aspect of the busy Welsh life of London which included, in around 1774, the establishment of a place of worship in Cock Lane, which grew into the famous Jewin chapel.

The fairs of the Midlands and London were not the only termini for the drovers. Again, according to R.J. Colyer, the herds were also driven to the Home Counties. Records show that Jenkin Williams of Deri Garon drove cattle to Blackwater in Kent while David Jonathan from Dihewyd sold cattle as far as Romford, Brentford, East Grinsted, Horsham and Kingston. Jonathan is an important example as he kept an account of all his business deals and expenses incurred during his various journeys between Cardiganshire and London. An example of his expenses is shown in Appendix 2.

All the drovers' roads that eventually led to London met

on the boundary around Hereford and then continued along the Edgeware Road to Smithfield, where the sales were held. Thence the cattle were driven to grazing areas where they were fattened for slaughter or used for a time for the developing milk market, with that milk having a very short shelf life. Then the drovers had to face the long trek home bringing with them tales from the city and of recent developments there.

Droving was dangerous work, especially when one considers that the money earned in the cattle trade was transported home by the head drover. Highway robbers were a danger, and eventually resulted in the drovers establishing a banking system. Some of them became very wealthy, for example, David Jones, who set up Banc yr Eidion Du (The Bank of the Black Ox) in Llandovery and then in Lampeter and Llandeilo. In 1909 the business was bought by Lloyds Bank. He was of farming stock and began working as a drover when only 15 years old. He married into money and that enabled him to set up the bank. When he died in 1879, he was worth £140,000.

Similar banks spread to other towns, notably the Aberystwyth and Tregaron Bank, or Banc y Ddafad Ddu (The Bank of the Black Sheep). It closed in 1815. It is fitting that the first such bank was established in Llandovery which was directly on the Drovers Road from Cardigan to Bercon as droving was the principal occupation of the area. Vicar Rhys Prichard (1579-1644) composed a poem of warning to the drovers as shown in Appendix 3. The first verse is typical of the nuance of the whole poem:

Os wyt borthmon dela'n onest
Tâl yn gywir am a gefaist
Cadw d'air, na thor addewid
Gwell nac aur mewn côd yw credid;

If you are a drover, deal honestly
Pay a fair price for what you get
Keep your word, do not break promises;
Better than gold is a code of ethics.

There were many temptations on the road as the drovers lodged in or near taverns. In London, at the end of the journey, the temptations of the town became the subject of many a sermon in the chapels and churches of Wales. Perhaps it was the result of hearing preachers in various services during and at the end of the journey that attracted the occasional drover away from the road to become a minister. R. J. Colyer in *The Welsh Cattle Drovers* refers to three such men. Benjamin Evans, a drover from Pembrokeshire, was ordained as a minister in Llanuwchllyn. William Jones from Trawsfynydd heard a sermon by the evangelist William Romaine (1714-1795) while on one of his journeys and became a minister. The best known was Dafydd Jones from Caeo (1711-1777). According to Gomer M. Roberts in his biography, Dafydd Jones learnt English while on his journeys between Caeo and London well enough to be able to translate several of Isaac Watts' hymns into Welsh. On his journeys also he heard some of John Welsey's open-air sermons and they interested him greatly. Dafydd Jones' hymns are full of symbolism connected with droving.

Fe ddeuant oll o'r dwyrain,
Gorllewin, Gogledd, De,
A Seion yn ddiatal,
Mae digon eto o le.

They gather from the East,
The West, the North and South,

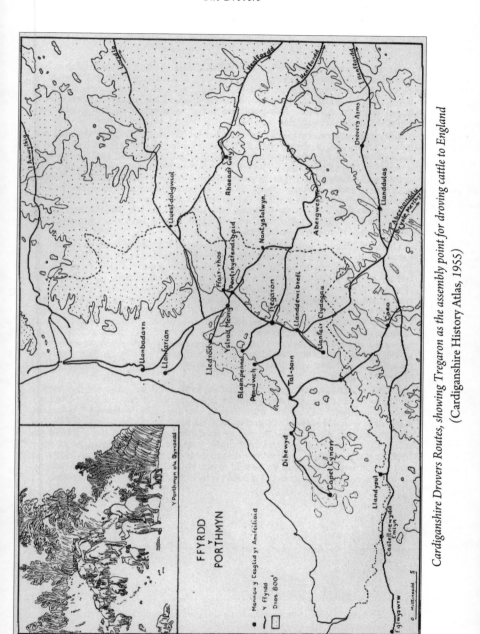

Cardiganshire Drovers Routes, showing Tregaron as the assembly point for droving cattle to England
(Cardiganshire History Atlas, 1955)

Two mid Wales drovers

Drovers' House, Stockbridge with a Welsh inscription on the wall:
'Gwair tymherus, porfa flasus, cwrw da a gwâl cysurus'.

From Zion all unchecked,
There's yet some room for more.

In his most famous hymn, 'Wele cawsom y Meseia' (Lo! We have the great Messiah) we see allusions to his trade as a cattle dealer:

Swm ein dyled fawr a dalodd
Ac fe groesodd filiau'r Ne'.

He settled the sum of our great debt
And crossed off our Heavenly bills.

And then:

Prynu'n bywyd, talu'n dyled
A'n glanhau â'i waed ei hun.

He bought our lives, paid our debts
And cleansed us with His blood.

His hymns abound with references to his life on the road. He writes: *Fe'm dwg i'r lleoedd da/ Lle tyf y borfa Nefol.* 'He bringeth me to the good places/ Where the heavenly pastures grow.' Then we have: *Arglwydd, arwain fi'n dy law, Na'd fi grwydro yma a thraw.* 'Lord, lead me with Thy hand/ Don't let me wander aimlessly.' And then: *Os af o'i ffyrdd yn ffôl/ Fy enaid nôl a eilw.* 'Should I foolishly wander from His paths, He will recall my soul.'

Evan Jones in his book on the old fairs refers to Dafydd Morris, a drover from Lledrod, who became a minister in Twrgwyn. He was the author of *Os gwelir fi, bechadur.* 'Should I, a sinner be seen.'

Many of the drovers developed a fluency in English and

that was a great advantage as they bargained across the border. There are at least two instances of drovers who became schoolteachers. In 1845, a school was opened in Pumpsaint by a drover. William Harris who was headmaster at Ffaldybrenin School from 1871-78 had spent some of his early years as a drover.

Not only did the drovers establish market and means for providing meat and milk, they also established smooth transit for the exiles from rural Wales to find different kinds of employment available in the city. It can be said that it was the drovers that kept the heart of rural Wales in direct contact with the metropolis.

Walking alongside the drovers on their travels were maids, some from the same districts as the drovers themselves. They helped in market places on the way to London and tended market gardens along the way. They would also look for domestic work. Their gardening included the task of weeding. As a result, they were known as 'chwynwyr' (weeders) and were referred to as such by the poet Daniel Evans from Cardiganshire:

> *O na bawn i fel colomen*
> *Ar ben Sant Paul yng nghanol Llunden*
> *I gael gweled merched Cymru*
> *Ar eu gliniau'n chwynnu gerddi.*

> How I wish I was a pigeon
> On St Paul's in the heart of London
> So I could see the girls from Wales
> Kneeling as they weed the gardens.

We have an account of the garden girls by John Williams-Davies in an issue of *Folk Life* in 1977. During the eighteenth and the beginning of the nineteenth century,

Tregaron and the nearby villages were the main centres for these girls. They were looked upon as tough and honest ladies, more so than the poor London girls, according to Williams-Davies. The London season extended from April to October and the Welsh girls had to compete for work with others from England and Ireland. While some of them stayed in London, many returned home at the end of the season and then returned to London year after year. It is said that one, from Llanddewibrefi, did so for twenty-one years without a break. The majority were daughters of smallholders they brought back earnings which were a great help in maintaining those smallholdings. According to Williams-Davies, even married women joined the crew.

These Garden Girls have contributed to modern Welsh literature. Mari Rhian Owen in a drama production, 'Merched y Gerddi' by Cwmni'r Arad Goch describes a journey undertaken by two of them who aspired to marrying into wealth. The play gives us an impression of contemporary work and wages. They earned three shillings an acre for hoeing, and three shillings and sixpence for weeding by hand.

Weavers and knitters would also walk with the drovers, woollen socks from Wales being very popular. The socks were sold from stalls that later developed, with Welsh names, into businesses that became well-known in London. Among them was Peter Jones, established in 1864, and is now under the John Lewis label. D.H. Evans went to London and opened a drapers shop now part of The House of Fraser.

All this travelling, particularly the droving, could cause considerable concern regarding Sunday observance. As late as 1896, John Evans, a drover from Anglesey, worrying at starting his journey on a Sunday, wrote in a letter to his wife:

I could not tell my children that I was going to London last Sunday, it would sadden their hearts. It would be no good telling my wife. It would only cause her to worry about how unlucky she had been in tying herself to such an un-Godly man.

Even a year later, in the *Gloucester Journal* of 4 August 1897, we read of two drovers found guilty of:

> ... defiling the Sabbath (ie Sunday) by driving cattle through the village of Mordiford in the County of Hereford. It is hoped that such illegal action will tend to stop such practices that have recently been too common and have proved to be very unpalatable to the keepers of the Sabbath.

Thus there were laws prohibiting droving on a Sunday. But the customs by now had begun to change substantially largely due to the coming of the railway at the middle of the nineteenth century. The line reached Aberystwyth in 1885 and Shrewsbury by 1864 creating a communication vein between Cardiganshire and the heart of London. This simplified the task of transporting livestock and lowered the cost substantially. It was also the line between Aberystwyth and Paddington that facilitated the huge exodus from Cardiganshire and on to the 'milky way' of London.

David Jones of Llanddewibrefi, who started work as a servant at eight years of age experienced droving cattle as well as exporting them by train to London. In the local community newspaper *Y Barcud* (Issue 7 1966) some of his experiences were recorded by his daughter, Jane Davies of Llwyn-y-groes. He went the first time, droving on foot, the cattle of his employer D. Griffiths of Y Ffrwd, Lampeter, a dealer who bought barren cows in Cardiganshire markets and some in Pembrokeshire. David Jones drove the herds to 'Gwlad y Gwair' (The Land of Grass), his name for Middlesex, undertaking the journey four times a year. In London he lodged in Shepherds Bush, paying the usual three pence a night and the equal sum for a breakfast of bread, cheese and tea. He said he could buy sufficient ale for four pence a quart. He recalled walking from Tregaron on to Abergwesyn heading for Hereford and onwards to Middlesex. He was accompanied by smiths carrying cues or metal shoes as well as nails and ropes to enable shoeing on the way. On one occasion there was an outbreak of Foot and Mouth Disease in Middlesex and he and the others were confined there for six weeks.

With the coming of the railway in the 1870s, he paid 18 shillings for a return ticket. But he was allowed to travel with the cattle free of charge. He spent his last working years accompanying sheep rather than cattle and died in 1950 aged 96.

Although the railway eventually brought an end to droving, the roads remain. There are appropriate names to record their existence. The drovers had regular calling places, and tavern names like Drovers Arms and Drovers Inn remain throughout Wales. Dafydd Jones of Caeo, the drover who became a minister, named his home Llundain Fach (Little London) and the nearby stream Tafwys (Thames). There are other London-based names surviving such as Temple Bar, Chancery, Hyde Park and many a Smithfield.

As for the shoeing areas, there exists close to Strata Florida remains of an old cottage called Pantcarnau (Hollow of the Hooves) where cattle were shod on their way over the mountain. And close to Llanbadarn Fawr there is a field still referred to as Cae Pedoli (Shoeing Field).

Even today, the former drovers' way near Southam just

over the boundary into England is known as the Welsh Road. It was so called as far back as 1755 as seen on old maps and especially on Tithe Maps from the mid nineteenth century. There is Welshman's Hill near Castle Bromwich and Welsh Meadow some three miles from Halesowen. Between Offchurch and Priors Hardwick there is Welsh Road Farm, Welsh Road Bridge, Welsh Road Meadow and Welsh Road Gorse.

It is apparent that the drovers' contribution is still remembered in many ways. One of the most lasting and interesting is the sign seen on the wall of a private the Drovers Inn in Stockbridge, Hampshire. This dates from the seventeenth century. The building, now a private house, is listed. The sign reads:

Gwair-tymherus-porfa-flasus-cwrw-da-a-gwâl-cysurus
Tempered-hay-tasty-grass-good-ale-and-comfortable-
beds

The drovers must have played an important part in all this. According to Professor Emrys Jones in his account The *Welsh in London*, by the coming of the railway the drovers had adjusted themselves to the great changes that had occurred and had become the pioneers of the milk trade as cattle keepers.

The Cow Keepers

As the railway network between Wales and England spread during the second part of the nineteenth century, so the traditional cattle trading continued, and as the population of London increased, so did the demand for milk. The market became more selective and knowledgeable. But this brought new difficulties.

The short shelf life of milk was the problem. Refrigeration did not exist and milk soon soured. The only means of extending the life of milk was by keeping it in cool places such as in cellars. Cattle had to be kept close by in order to secure an adequate and regular supply.

Some cattle keepers held grazing right on common land near their homes but the majority of animals were kept in places varying from cellars to lofts. Some were kept in garrets to which cattle were hoisted by ropes. They were then kept until they ceased producing milk or until their yield became too scant to be of value, then they were slaughtered and replaced with fresh animals.

By 1871, as much as 72 per cent of London's milk was supplied from the city's cowsheds and according to David Taylor, in his book *London's Milk Supply 1885-1900*, there were then as many as 24,000 cattle in the capital. He adds that one milkman, a Mr Rhodes of Islington, kept on average 400 milking cows. Most common yards held some 50 – 80 animals on farms within reach of the city though the smaller farms usually kept no more than a dozen or so milking cows.

It is impossible to gauge exactly how many of London's cow keepers were Welsh during the seventeenth and eighteenth century. However, Welsh surnames in parish registers indicate that the Welsh were there in numbers. Between 1840 and 1892, around Whitechapel alone, a number of Welsh people and their relatives are listed as having connections with keeping cattle and selling milk. For example, in Black Lion Yard in Commercial Road are found Hugh Evans of Bethania, his wife Jane from Penuwch and daughter Elizabeth; Magdalene James, Llangwyryfon; John Evans, Llanfihangel-y-creuddyn and his wife Mary Jane; Morgan Griffiths, nephew; William Evans, Llangeitho; Margaret Morris, Pennant; and George Gregory, Llanddeiniol. It is believed that the Evans family had connections with the milk trade until the Great War. The next owner was another Welshman, William Jones from around Aberystwyth; he kept between twenty and forty cows. The business reverted then to another Evans, Joshua Evans. He kept the cattle until the end of the war but continued to run the business until 1949.

Another way of assessing the number of Welsh in London, not necessarily from Cardiganshire, was by tracing the number and percentage of the relevant surnames as the nineteenth century developed. The following statistics were supplied by Peter Atkins, Professor of Geography at Durham University:

Date	Cow Keeper	Welsh Surname	Percentage
1881	998	240	24
1890	285	116	41
1900	168	82	49
1910	102	47	46

The decrease in numbers over 30 years can be attributed to changes in the ways of marketing milk, from keeping cattle and milking on the premises to receiving milk transported by train. But the Welsh more than held their own during this time of change, as the near doubling in their presence, in terms of percentage, clearly shows.

The Welsh were the backbone of the industry and they were the only ones who succeeded. In 1904, Charles Booth published 'Report on Life and Labour in London 1886 – 1903'. What he has to say about the milk trade interesting. The Welsh, he says, were the only people to succeed.

> They alone from among the United Kingdom's inhabitants are able to make keeping cattle in London pay; or rather they alone are able to accept the conditions under which cattle keepers are compelled to live and work under in order to make a living. They are, in the majority, of low education; have an imperfect grasp of English ... They are frugal and self-denying, living under harsh conditions, working extremely hard for unusually long hours and for very little financial return.

During the early part of the nineteenth century, it was customary to milk in public, and straight into the bowl or jug. The cattle were kept in common cow-houses and then led out to public areas for milking thus taking the milk directly to the buyer. For example, in St James' Park there were places where the cattle could be tethered and 16milked directly into the customer's vessels on the spot.

During the 1860s, eight cows continued to be kept in the park during the summer and four in the winter, as was the custom for this method of direct milking. Later on in the century, all milk not sold over the counter was distributed by milkmaids who carried fifteen gallons of milk on yokes carried on their shoulders in open buckets. They could be heard shouting 'Milko! Milko!' The customers brought their jugs with them and the milkmaids would ladle the milk into the jugs. This method was, of course, subject to contamination. In 1818, a detailed description was provided

Milking cows kept by the Welsh, 19th century
(Glyn Lewis collection)

A Welsh milkmaid carrying milk in a yoke, early 19th century
(Glyn Lewis collection)

by an unknown contemporary author of the girls who
carried the milk buckets:

> The milk in tin buckets was carried mainly by strong and
> sturdy Welsh girls ... These are the girls who also sell
> the milk on the city streets and it is unbelievable seeing
> the labour and tiredness suffered by these girls and the
> jollity and cheerfulness that is typical of them that tends,
> in a strange way, to lighten their heavy work ... The
> weight they are used to carrying on their yokes, for
> example, over a distance of three miles is between 100
> and 130 pounds. By mid-day they would have returned
> to the cow keepers to collect more milk before returning
> to the street until six o clock. For this they would be paid
> nine shillings a week and their breakfast.
>
> The milkmaid would have a regular round of
> customers, or her 'milk walk' ... Some would be
> travellers who would shout their wares whilst looking for
> customers. Their calls of 'Milk below' sounded like
> 'Mio'.

The cattle were fed grain from nearby breweries. They were
also provided with clean straw and vegetables from the
markets. One can only imagine what was done with their
excrement! We have at least one explanation. Ieuan Parry
from Blaenplwyf recalls his father telling him that it was
carried along the Thames in open barges drawn by horses
and then used in Surrey gardens as a fertilizer. It was there
that some of the girls referred to earlier as weeders worked.

Because of the competition between some of the milk-
sellers, advertising was crucial. We find flowery adverts
boasting of their products. A typical advert by E.J. Walker of
40 Sloane Street can be seen in 'Kelly's Directory' in 1910. It
maintains that it could supply milk from its cow herds to its

Milk churns arriving in Paddington, early 20th century
(Glyn Lewis collection)

Milk churns in a Welsh station waiting for the train to London
(Glyn Lewis collection)

customer's doorsteps within three hours of milking. It also claimed that the milk was free of TB and therefore particularly suitable for babies and the sick. Another claim was that the ventilation, the lighting and the hygiene arrangements were perfect. That implies no smell of cow manure!

In 1865, herds were infected with Rindepest Disease, or Cattle Pest. In fact the sickness was a combination of *rindepest* and *pleuropneumonia* combined with a strain of Foot and Mouth Disease. This was not a result of poor hygiene but rather a viral infection. Despite the losses, it led to the cleansing of the milk industry – basic hygiene standards were established and also certificated inspections that could be used to promote milkmen's businesses. Licensing cattle-keeping centres limited the number of animals that could be kept. The qualifications were shown on official documents such as billheads, showing that the company was under the supervision of the London County Council. One business that reflected this on its billheads was Jones' Dairy in Spitalfields on which was recorded the number of cattle the establishment was entitled to keep.

Rindepest proved to be the turning point in the development of dairying, and consequently in milk provision in London. The heavy losses resulting from the cattle disease meant that there would have been a severe shortage of milk were it not for the consignments that arrived by train from the farms and areas around the London stations. It is estimated that some seven million gallons of milk were transported into London by train during 1886 to fill the gap in the production of the city dairies affected by the disease. It is interesting to note the emergence of Express Dairies in particular. It emanated directly from the incidence of Rindepest Disease when George Barham started a new milk supplying business. It was the very fact that the milk was transported to London by train that led to the venture being named Express Dairies. This was followed by United Dairies, The Independent Milk Suppliers and the Co-op. In 1959 United Dairies and Cow and Gate merged to form Unigate.

Despite all the changes, the supply of milk from local cowsheds continued. However, the different sources led to a variation in supply and price. As a result of the Agricultural Marketing Law the Milk Marketing Board was established in 1933. Its aim was to regulate milk marketing through the Board buying all the milk produced and then selling it for consumption or to make various milk products. All the income was then dispersed among producers according to the amounts sold by them to the Board.

The business of cattle keeping dwindled during the nineteenth century but enjoyed a revival with the advent of Jewish immigration into the East End between 1881 and

E. J. Walker cow-keeping advert, with claims of purity and cleanliness
(Kensington Central Library)

Short Horn Dairy, J. T. G. Price's business, 1897
(Glyn Lewis collection)

1914. The Jews had their own Kosher dietary rules. As part of these customs it was necessary that cows should be milked in the presence of someone from the Jewish community, a Rabbi or Shomer. To ensure purity, it was also required for the cows to be milked directly into the customer's personal container. Those of strictly Jewish faith queued for their supply of milk and this carried a premium of two pence a pint.

A new generation of cattle keepers appeared, many from West Wales, people driven from the land by financial exigencies. They brought with them their husbandry skills as had earlier immigrants. One of the better known was William Jones, Black Lion Yard, Stepney. He was able to converse in Yiddish to his customers but spoke Welsh to his sons. He conscientiously kept and respected the Jewish customs and thus gained the respect of the community. He owned a herd of forty cattle which were milked for six months before being slaughtered and exchanged. His successor in the business, Jos Evans milked the herd in the presence of a Rabbi until the end of the war, finally leaving London in 1949..

However, as the Jewish population of the East End moved on, the demand for Kosher milk subsided. By 1936, only thirty six cattle keepers remained with 151 cows; by 1940 there were sixteen keepers and by 1950, only two. One of those, John Jordan, who represented the fourth generation of cattle keepers in Peckham (although not officially in the East End) remained until 1967 keeping between thirty and forty cows.

If demand exceeded supply, it would be necessary to buy from a wholesaler. Following the bombing during World War II and the effects of the TB regulations, as well as economic factors, the last cow left the East End in 1954. The last of the keepers was David Carsons who kept cattle near Tower Bridge.

A renewed call for Kosher milk came in 1939-45 as Jews fled from Nazi prosecution in Europe. Evan Jones, now of Llanddewibrefi, and whose parents came from Cellan and Lampeter before leaving for London in 1931, moving to Staines in 1938, recalled his parents supplying a population of strictly Orthodox Jews. Some of them had returned to their homelands after the war. Later, Hungarian Jews had to seek refuge from the Russians in 1956, and Evans' parents met the need for Kosher milk once more.

Towards the end of the nineteenth century, much of the milk produced by cows in London was advertised as high quality produce in an attempt to protect the city cow keepers from produce reaching London by train. The decline in demand for city-produced milk and the increasing dependency on 'train milk' sparked a lively debate in the press regarding their relative qualities. The *Aberdare Leader* in January 1870 maintained that the cream quality of city milk was superior whilst the *County Observer and Monmouth Central Adviser* on 4 March 1876 insisted that the perils of dangerous impurities was much higher on country farms than in the old cowsheds of London. Also there was greater danger of adulteration by adding water. This can be compared to today's debate over genetic engineering. Whatever the argument for or against 'railway milk', the implementation of a progressive and stricter public health regime in the twentieth century ensured a supply of healthier and cleaner milk.

Indications of the sites of cattle keepers are still to be found. Buildings used to house cattle frequently displayed a carving of a cow's head on their outer walls. Five of these have survived including one on the corner of Kings Road and Smith Street. Another can be seen in Old Church Street. An article published by Camden Council commemorates the home of Thomas Edwards who kept cattle there in no 61 Marchmont Street, Bloomsbury. Today it is a café providing internet service. Cattle in city cowsheds have even featured in paintings. Robert Hill (1769-1844) painted a watercolour in 1822, A Cowhouse in Marylebone Park', a painting now part of a private collection.

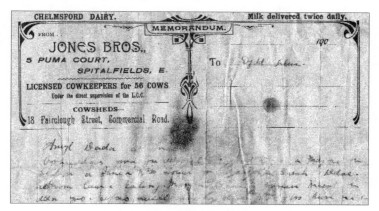

Memo Heading Spitalfields Dairy (Emyr Humphreys)

Cows who walked the walk in Toronto
(David and Margaret Wells)

It is worth adding a postscript. On the wall of a restaurant in Toronto, Canada, there is a reminder of a time when this place too must have been a shop selling milk to meet the needs of the locals in the same way as the London shops did during the same period. Customers are reminded of the way cattle were hoisted up into attics, where they would be kept for milking. On the wall outside and under the sign is a full-sized image of two cows, the rear end of one and the fore end of another. They had certainly walked the walk!

Fate and Favour

In the *Welsh Gazette* of February 1928 there appears an account of the wedding of a young couple from South Cardiganshire who planned to go to London to join the milk trade. The two last sentences were:

> *Mae y par ifanc wedi cychwyn masnach eu hunain yn y drafnidiaeth llaeth yn Llundain. Dymunwn iddynt y ffafr a'r ffawd sy'n canlyn pawb ar y llwybr llaethog.*

> The young couple have started their own milk marketing business in London. We wish them the grace and favour that befalls all on the milky way.

The author of these words was Isfoel, one of the Cilie brothers. The Cilie, Cwmtydu, family were farmers, sea captains and ministers of religion who contributed much to Welsh cultural life in the twentieth century. Isfoel was a farmer and a poet. What is interesting in his words is that this is not mere sentimental well-wishing but rather a presumption of success. That is, if one became a part of the milk business, there would be no question of failure. A few months later the groom's father wrote as follows:

> *Yr oedd yn dda gennyf glywed fod y lle newydd wedi troi maes yn ddymunol a bod Leisa Jane wedi gwerthu mwy na'r rhai o'i blaen. Fod tithau Daniel wedi cadw y cwsmeriaid i gyd. Gobeithio y parhaith hi yn y blaen a bod yr arian yn dod mewn yn neis.*

One is glad to hear that the new place has turned out well and that Leisa Jane has sold more than her predecessors. Also that you, Daniel have retained all the customers. Let us hope it continues thus and that the money will come in nicely.

The young couple were my prospective parents. Reading between the lines, one discovers references to life in the old country – that is hard work and the need to be careful with money. One imagines that the first business, in common with all that ventured, was a terrace shop though the aim would be for a corner shop with more direct access to the source of business, customers. There was no collateral to persuade a bank to lend money. Rather, the necessary loan would be made by a relative, more often than not, a Cardi relative who had himself succeeded in business. This was typical of his fellow countrymen. Another means of obtaining collateral was by obtaining a friend's financial backing or by selling family possessions in Wales.

Iwan Jones of Lampeter is an example of the first instance. In 1931 his father borrowed £1,100 from the bank without a corresponding warrant, but the loan was underwritten by a friend. In the second instance, Dilys Scott from Felinfach's parents had to sell their business, Cwmcarfan Mill in order to purchase a milk business in Southall. In my parents' case, they borrowed money from my father's brother; he was single and was considerably older than my father. The money was borrowed on condition that his brother would receive a specific rate of interest on his loan. Should the venture fail, my father would only have to repay the sum he had borrowed.

The only other source, if the first two options failed, was to gain the support of one of the large wholesale milk companies. The disadvantage, of course, was that the lender would then be dependent upon the company for his milk supply. Then, market conditions worsened, the wholesalers would cease lending money to the individual milkman who needed it as a payment for the business' goodwill. According to Emrys Davies from Brynaman (originally from Cellan) that was the beginning of the end of the independent milk businesses in London.

As can be seen, goodwill and business interests were crucial. The extent of the goodwill depended upon the income that could be generated from the business as it stood at the time of the agreement. The aim was to increase the income and thus the value (that is, the goodwill) of the business. As can be seen in the Appendices, agreement would be reached based on either the size of the milk business at what was purchased from the wholesalers, or the produce of the cattle kept on the site. Income from the shop was also a consideration. Included in the agreement was the promise to 'buy on the basis of fair evaluation at the time of completion of sale all stock and goods available for sale.' That included the cattle if appropriate.

The purchase would be administered by an agent, almost certainly a Welshman, who specialised in this kind of work. Following are the bare bones of two Agreements typical in the buying of the goodwill, that is, a measure of the business' value.

In 1936, Llew and Jane Evans bought the goodwill of a business in Fulham (see Appendix 4). It was noted that the business retailed 25 gallons of milk per day for seven pence a quart together with shop goods to the value of £25 per week (some £1,500 today). The purchase price in the Agreement was £750 (some £44,800 today). The seller undertook 'not to set up exercise or be concerned in setting up or carrying the trade or business of a Retail Milk Vendor or provision dealer ... within a radius of two miles of the premises for a period of ten years following the completion of the purchase.' The book debts, (money on the slate) would be bought at a discount of 15 percent. If they were not bought, the seller agreed not to press the customers for payment for such debts for two months following the purchase. That, probably, was intended to continue the goodwill of the business. The purchase price also included the acquisition of business installations, the furniture and the utensils that were part of the business.

A similar Agreement was drawn in 1919 when Rees Edwards (see Appendix 5) sold a business in Rotherhithe to Daniel Lloyd. The price was £825 (£36,000 today). This was for a sale of 70 gallons of milk daily to *bona fide* customers for one shilling a quart. Also 70 gallons for a shilling a quart less 10 gallons a day for 11 pence a quart on an average of a seven day week. Here, the counter trade was £80 per week (£3,830 today) including the milk sold in the shop but excluding the milk sold outside. (The monetary comparisons are based on *Money.co.uk* but these estimates can vary).

Here again the sellers were required 'not to establish or help establish a business selling milk or goods ... within a radius of two miles ... or to serve any customer involved with the said Business for a period of ten years'. In both instances the buyer was entitled to be trained in the business for seven days prior to and after the purchase.

Following the terms of Agreement, a list of the possessions that would remain on the site was drawn up:

Dairy	Shop
Two prams	Two external blinds
Two brass churns	Marble butter block
Two Hand Cans and marble top	Wallmirrors
Six Measures	One pair of scales
One 16 quart bucket measure	Set of Brass Measures up to 2lbs
One plunger	Earthenware Counter Vessel
One Gallon Measure	White Metal Lids

One Measuring Drum	Set of Wooden Butter Shaper
	All Filling
Lawrence Cooler, Drum	Two Egg Globes
Two Cans	

A plunger, incidentally, was a type of ladle for stirring the milk before bottling to ensure that the milk and cream were thoroughly blended.

It was noted that in both cases the purchases concerned 'had been fairly priced … and all goods and stock of the trade.'

The goodwill of a business was priced on Marketing Accounts and Profit and Loss data prepared by an accountant a year prior to the sale. One still exists pertaining to the business of D.R. and Miss E.E. Daniel. The details are as follows overleaf.

The net profit today would be £28.600 with £47,000 gross profit.

The Declaration of Agreement followed. Here we will make do with two examples: Bowen Williams' family sold their business after returning to Wales in 1921, a business registered as 'Cowkeepers and Retail Business'. Also there exists a Declaration of Agreement concerning a business sold by Roscoe Lloyd in 1933, probably a dairy minus cattle. (The Agreements are seen in Appendices 6 and 7).

Obviously, a good head for figures was needed. In his article 'The Land of Milk and Honey' which appeared in the *Western Mail* in 1988, Gwyn Griffiths claims that a typical London Cardi's reading consisted of three books: the Bible, the denominational hymn book and *The Ready Reckoner*. Also one had to be able to 'add up' when noting various sales at the end of the day, before calculators and bar codes had ever been heard of.

Trading and Profit Loss Account for the period 23rd March 1931 – 2nd April 1932

Dr.		Cr.	
To stock as at 23rd March 1931	£130-0-0	By Takings	£4007–15-8
To Purchases	£3,265-12-10	By Stock as at 2nd April 1932	£190-8–10
To Gross Profit c/d	£802–11-8		
	£4,198-4-6		£4,198-4-6
To Rent	£60-0-0	By Gross Profit	£802–11-8
To Rates	£29–17-0		
To Lighting and Heating	£20-13-0		
To Telephone	£12-3-9		
To Wages	£120-18-0		
To Dairy Requisites	£18-10-8		
To Repairs	£24-2-2		
To Insurances	£11-17-3		
To Sundries	£19-3-3		
To Net Profit	£485-6-7		
	£802–11-8		£802–11-8

I certify that I have prepared the foregoing from the Books of Mr. D. E. and miss E.E. Daniel and that the same is correct and in correct and in accordance therein to the best of my knowledge and belief.

Signed by certified accountant

Daniel and Margaret Jones with one of their maids in their shop
(Edwin Jones, Cross Inn, Llannon)

Roscoe Lloyd and colleague with two Welsh Cobs in Acton, early 1930s
(Ifor and Myfanwy Lloyd)

When and where a cattle-keeping and milking location at a particular location ended, milk was supplied from rural farms. Produce from cows milked twice a day was cooled and strained on the farm and then poured in bulk into churns and transported to roadsides. There the churns were placed on stands level with the beds of the milk lorries that collected them and taken to milk factories like Pont Llanio in Cardiganshire. From these factories the milk was transported on milk trains, part of the Great Western Railway network serving the agricultural countryside of West Wales.

The milk was then taken to central creameries where it was pasteurised, poured into 17 gallon churns and distributed to the retailing dairy businesses. The early churns were cone-shaped to avoid tipping over; they had mushroom-shaped lids and strong bases to make them easier to tilt and roll. In the dairies the milk was bottled manually or with the aid of a machine into quart, pint or half-pint bottles which would then be capped, and all bearing the dairy's logo.

The bulk of milk sold was pasteurised. This entailed heating milk to a temperature of 75.5 degrees Centigrade for between 15 and 20 seconds, thus killing the bacteria without having an effect on the quality or taste of the milk. Sterilised milk, or 'ster' colloquially was milk that had been preheated to 50 degrees Centigrade, homogenised, bottled, sealed and then reheated to a higher temperature for between 10 and 20 minutes. As a result it changed taste and colour, but it was popular as it had an extended shelf life. Grade A milk was also available as well as Channel Island milk, richer in cream. After World War II, the milk arrived ready bottled from the creameries.

The milk had to be on the doorstep before seven o'clock in time for breakfast. There was always a later second round

Buildings still showing evidence of cow-keeping in years past

The site of an old Welsh Dairy, Old Church Street, Chelsea

The site of the old cowshed, dairy and the maids and servants' quarters at the back. The cow's head is still to be seen on many former dairy walls.

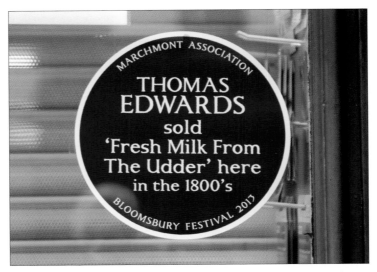

Thomas Edwards' former dairy shop, 61 Marchmont Street, Bloomsbury

Another dairy to be seen on King's Road, Chelsea

Jones Brothers

W.A.Evans & Son

R.Evans & Son

Rees Price Dairies

I.Jones

E.P.Davies

Morgans Hygienic
Dairy

Edwards Dairy Farms
Ltd

Bottle tops from some of the Welsh companies
(Glyn Lewis collection)

DARWIN FARM DAIRY

E. DAVIES & SONS
(DAIRIES) LTD.

Purveyors of
High - Class Dairy Produce
ALL GRADES OF MILK SUPPLIED
Best Dairy Butter. New-Laid Eggs a speciality

Agents for
WALL'S ICE CREAM and BIRDS EYE FROSTED FOODS

Under strict medical and sanitary supervision

52 DARWIN STREET · OLD KENT ROAD
Phone : RODney 3513

Telephone : WATerloo 4721

LEWIS'S DAIRIES
(Proprietor: W. L. LEWIS)

All Milk Pasteurised and Bottled on the premises

9-11 POCOCK STREET
BLACKFRIARS ROAD, S.E.1

ESTABLISHED
FIFTY YEARS.

NON-
COMBINE.

Just . . . . .
PURE MILK
. . . That's all

T. CHARLES
1 Hamilton St., Deptford, S.E. 8

OWEN & SON

Dairymen

Pure Clean Milk — Supplied Twice Daily.
Daily Arrivals of English New Laid Eggs.

249, CAMBERWELL NEW RD.

E. MORRIS & SONS
Ossory Dairy

Families supplied with Pure Milk & Cream
direct from the Farm twice daily
NOTED FOR NURSERY MILK
AND NEW LAID EGGS

462, Old Kent Rd., S.E. 1

D. WILLIAMS

Cardigan Farm Dairy

PURE CLEAN MILK DIRECT
FROM FARMS IN WILTS
AND SOMERSET.

Milk can be obtained any hour
at night from our Automatic
Milk Supply.

51, WYNDHAM ROAD,
CAMBERWELL, S.E.

Welsh dairy advertisements
(Glyn Lewis collection)

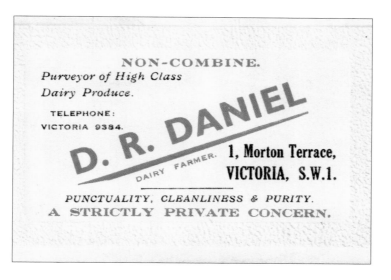

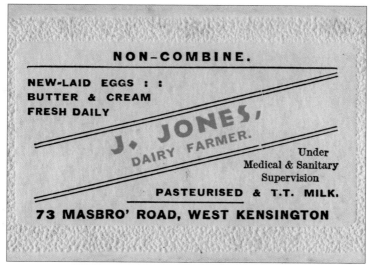

Welsh dairy business cards

Combermere Road about 1932 (Richard and Jois Snelson)

Ted Hughes and Jois Snelson (Roberts), Bramley Road
(Richard and Jois Snelson)

Businesses with Welsh roots still remaining

Jones Bros., Middlesex Street, City of London Dairy

John and Edward Lewis, of Lewis Bros. Dairies

A fleet of Morgan Dairy vans, Fulham

Shop fronts still retaining their earlier daily life

*The former Lloyd's Dairy, on the corner of River Street and Amwell Street,
now a barber shop*

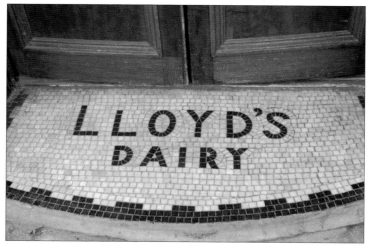

The old tiles on the doorstep can still be seen

The interior of the Lloyd's Dairy
as it was in 1994

Dairy 'equipment' (Margaret Thomas)

One of Jones Brothers,
Bramley Road's milk bottles
(Aled Jones)

Erstwhile milk shop with listed building status

The former John Evans Dairy, 35 Warren Street
with the passageway to the cowshed nearby

The business is now run by Turkish people.
The building retains many of its old features.

The Pugh family in their Oxford Express Dairy in Frith Street, Soho before deciding to call it a day

Mary Bott's family outside their Kilburn shop
(Mary Bott)

T. H. Jones' shop in Clapham Junction
(Hywel and Elinor Thomas)

John Jones and employee outside their Masbro Road, Kensington, shop
(Edwin Jones)

W. Evans Dairy in 130 St John Street, Clerkenwell
(Margaret Humphreys, Machynlleth)

A Cranbrook Dairy barrow and roundsman (Alun Eirug Davies)

*The family of French's Dairy, Rigby Street, outside their shop in 1947
(Maggie Owen)*

The owners of Fairlawn Dairy outside their shop
(Evan Jones)

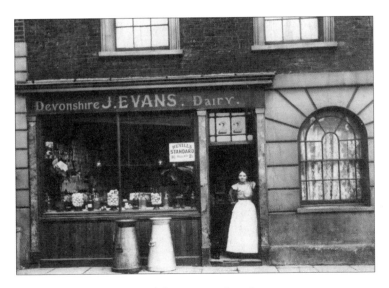

J. Evans' dairy, Devonshire Dairy
(Elgan Davies)

known by some as 'the pudding delivery', and in some instances even a third delivery. The milk was delivered in prams or carts, also known as barrows, pushed or pulled manually; later they were battery powered. As well as milk, the carts carried a full complement of dry goods from the shop. On return the cart stock was counted back in, sales noted and the empty bottles washed and sterilised with hot water and soda and then placed bottoms up to drain.

A constant problem for the small businesses was the arranging of a rota of delivery men for the rounds so that they could claim the right of a day off despite the demands of milk supply. Bowen Williams, having 50 years' experience from 1932, can describe a complicated plan that he himself contrived in order to persuade customers to accept a two-day supply occasionally on set days. Furthermore, the business owner had to be on hand to replace a worker absent due to illness or otherwise. In one business one finds a roundsman from Wales prepared to work on Saturday so that his Jewish fellow workers could observe their holy day. The Jews returned the favour so that the Welsh roundsmen could attend chapel on Sundays.

The shop was open seven days a week from early morning till late at night. There was early closing on Sunday, and on either Wednesday or Thursday. However it was often necessary for the shopkeeper to answer to a knock on the door from a forgetful customer. Goodwill had to be maintained.

The day's work didn't end when the shop door was closed. Stock had to be checked and the shelves refilled. Unlike today, cheese did not arrive in tidy packages of various sizes. There were only two kinds, strong and mild; it arrived in large rolls wrapped in cotton weave and then had to be divided into convenient pieces. Pre-war, eggs arrived in oblong boxes from various countries, some from England

i. *Mayfield Farm Dairies; ii. Dorset dairy; each indicating the emphasis on*
purity, punctuality and personal service
(i. Eleri Davies; ii Evana Lloyd)

Butter wrapping paper with shop's logo
(Ceredigion Museum)

and others from Denmark, Holland and Middle Europe and all advertised as Fresh Eggs. Post war, they came from more local sources. Cambridgeshire supplied two dairies at least.

Butter and lard came in half hundredweight packs and then had to be divided into packs of either a half or a quarter pound wrapped in greaseproof paper bearing the shop's logo. At the end of the week, every customer's bill was prepared. Some of these bills displayed claims not seen today. Mayfield Farm Dairies claimed:

> **Scrupulous cleanliness. Rigorous punctuality.**
> **Families waited on three times daily.**
> **Under Medical supervision**

On Dorset's Dairy's bills, where they boasted that they sold pure milk, was written:

> **Quality guaranteed and your recommendation**
> **respectfully solicited**

Betty Davies from Aberporth's family worked in the East End. They kept eight cows in a cowshed in the yard behind their home as well as chickens. This meant they could claim in the local advertiser:

> **D.J. Williams, Dairyman**
>
> **Purest milk money can buy**
>
> **Best pure butter**
>
> **New laid Eggs from our own farm**

The centre and heart of the business where all the administration took place was the room behind the shop, or

London Wholesale Dairies Thames trip for milk retailers, early 1930s
(Megan Hayes)

the shop parlour. Here, the weekly bills were prepared item by item. Any business which did not have an associated milk round was known as an 'indoor dairy'.

The appearance of the shop was of paramount importance. The shop window was dressed weekly, a common feature being an arrangement of tins in a pyramid shape. The decorations could include Blackamoor figurines kneeling and holding baskets full of eggs. My parents had such a figure and one could be seen in Gwen Manley's family's shop in City Road. Today, of course, such figurines are not politically correct.

The counter servers wore white starched overalls. The men on the milk rounds wore ankle-length aprons with lightly coloured horizontal stripes.

Great emphasis was placed on the customer's personal preference, possible because each was known personally: for instance, a customer might wish to have her lard or butter in plain grease-proof paper so that it could re-used for making steamed pudding. Some dairies offered a Christmas present of cream to customers, how much being dependent on the custom and possibly regularity of bill settlement. If a customer happened to be away, they could be forward enough to ask for it to be delivered on their return.

Sometimes, country practices proved useful for city work. Roscoe Lloyd and his wife Elin from South Cardiganshire went to London after their marriage in 1938 and started a business in Acton Lane before moving to Chiswick. He delivered milk from a cart drawn by two Welsh Cobs. Roscoe – father of singers Ifan and Ifor Lloyd – could train a cob within a fortnight to traverse the round in such a way that the cobs would stop outside every house to enable delivery before proceeding and stopping outside the next house in turn, and that without any bidding.

Not only were Welsh agents central to all transactions relating to the transfer of a business, but the purchaser would set about to display signs noting that the business continued under Welsh ownership. They displayed their names at once above the door and shop window. Elgan Davies' father in Tottenham sold his business to a Morgan family. They, in turn, sold the business to a family called Evans. Their names, in turn, were displayed with pride. The shop windows advertised their produce, Grade 'A' milk and 'Neville's Standard Bread' and so on.

While shop owners' names were displayed proudly, business names were, more often than not, English. For instance, my parents' business in Clapham was known as Roseneath Dairy and in Richmond as Vicarage Farm Dairy. But some owners prided themselves in naming their businesses in Welsh. D.R. and E. Daniels' dairy in Pimlico was named Glasfryn Dairy. Roscoe Lloyd called his premises Aeron Dairy while Jois Snelson's family kept the Garth Dairy in Bramley Road. One wonders whether these names were connected with the original Welsh establishers?

The majority ventured into the milk trade after a period

working in an already established concern. Even so, Evan and Carol Evans, today living in Tal-y-bont, took the plunge without any prior experience immediately after their marriage in 1964. That took courage, but they benefited from a clause in their agreement which decreed that that the vendor should support the purchasers for a set period. Thanks to hard work they succeeded after ten years to sell the business to a couple from Carmarthenshire.

Peggy Beaven clearly remembers her parents, John and Margaret Jacob's shop in Willesden. Her mother would wash the milk bottles in a tub and the milk was delivered on a bike or pram. She remembers not only the usual pint, half pint and quart but also milk by the gill, a third of a pint. Milk and butter were kept cold by being kept on a marble counter. Once, her father decided to place the butter under a window above the shop doorway in order to keep it cool. Unfortunately a thief broke in through the window and landed with his feet in the butter. The eggs were stored in a wooden box lined with straw and one of the most popular of goods were broken biscuits.

Lewis Lloyd, son of Moss Lloyd one of the Esgairgarn children, Llanddewibrefi in the twenties remembers his parents using a large wooden box as a cooler; blocks of ice delivered once a month were placed on the box to keep the goods within cool.

Often the maids and servants were chosen from the home area of the shop owners back in Wales. These could be girls who wished to take a year off before commencing their career or older women wishing to spend a year in the big city before settling down. They would be recruited by advertising in the local paper such as the *Welsh Gazette,* or by personal contact and recommendation of a friend or relative from home and lived as family members undertaking all the work and duties associated with running the business. Two such in our family were Norah Morgan from Caerwedros, who later worked as a Health Visitor in her native village and Bet Davies from Cwmsychpant, who later farmed Blaenhirbant Uchaf.

Norah Morgan, Caerwedros who worked with my family in Clapham

Mary Jones, now from Ammanford tells how the owners of one business, Bonner's Dairy, Piccadilly employed only maids from their village, Cwmllynfell. As a result, several of their family members worked there, her mother, her aunt as well as friends from the area, one after another. These again lived in, and under strict supervision which included regular compulsory chapel attendance. This was comparable to the employer operating 'in loco parentis' and undertaking the parental care and duty of the girls' parents.

The milkmen created a loose network. If it was known that a customer was leaving to live in an area outside the designated two-mile limit, a phone call would result in a pint of milk being placed on their doorstep to tempt their custom.

Bet Davies, Cwmsychbant who worked with my family in Richmond

Pride was part of the milkman's being and part of that

Metropolitan Dairymen's Association Dinner, 1930s
(Hywel and Elinor Thomas)

The Morgan family shop – with Blackamoor statue in the window display
(Gwen Manley)

pride was ensuring that, come what may, the milk would be delivered to the householder. During the General Strike of 1926, delivery of milk to individual dairies ceased. Instead, there was a bulk delivery to Hyde Park. There, individual milk merchants collected their supply to be delivered to customers on their rounds. Even during the severe winter of 1947, deliveries were made, often by using a sled instead of a cart. One who remembers this vividly is Elizabeth Evans.

Today, the ephemera of the milk trade are valued by individual collectors. One can purchase on the web items such as milk bottles and cardboard caps displaying the names and logos of the various dairies.

The majority of milk men belonged either to the Metropolitan Dairymen's Association or the Amalgamated Master Dairymen. These helped prevent the spread of comprehensive businesses and encouraged cooperation between the smaller businesses by the organising of various social events. In the early twenties, trips along the Thames were organised by the London Wholesale Dairies.

The general picture is one of a population wishing to escape the poverty of their home areas in Cardiganshire and elsewhere. These were people who were prepared to work hard and to offer help to their fellow exiles whilst remaining completely faithful to the land of their birth.

Family Ties

The exodus to London tended to be family affairs. It was customary for members of the same family to follow each other and thus create a lineage of milk people.

Families during this period were large. Educational opportunities were few. An occasional Cardiganshire family at the end of the nineteenth century and early in the twentieth strove to ensure an education for their offspring in the numerous preparatory schools and, if possible, in one of the training or theological colleges. Alan Leech's biography of Dan Jenkins, Pentrefelin, Tal-sarn clearly reflects the educational situation in Cardiganshire. Even so, more frequently than not, education was the privilege of the eldest son; as a result, the education of the younger members of the predominately large families was limited. The choice for boys was to await tenancy, to go west for a life at sea (a calling that was traditional close to the sea shores) depart for the coalmines of the South or to go east to pursue a trade established by the drovers and continued by the cattle keepers. Girls could only seek to go into service until they found a husband.

The attractions of London were very tempting despite the fact that the exiles' knowledge of English was very sparse due to Welsh being the native tongue of the Cardiganshire countryside. The great majority were monoglot Welsh. Further on we read how Ann Jones from Bronnant departed for London with her parents when only twelve years old and having no English apart from the odd phrase of greeting and thanks. She was by no means alone in this respect, Furthermore, however fluent the English, there was the problem of mastering the local dialect How on earth could a Welsh speaking immigrant be expected to understand that 'three ha'pence' meant the same as the phrase for 'penny halfpenny'?

To ease such difficulties, the families tended to work in family groups or at least to send someone ahead to prepare the ground and await the others. Mrs Olwen Jones' grandfather, of Lampeter, was one of twelve children, eleven of whom headed for London. From a family of ten from Pantyblawd Farm in Llanddewibrefi, five went to London. Then four from the Cryncoed family of Derwen Gam. Five members of the Crynfryn-bychan, Llwynpiod family left home at the beginning of the twentieth century to work in the London milk trade and later succeeded as owners in different areas of the city. In such matters they reflected what is described by Gwyneth Francis Jones in *Cows, Cardis and Cockneys*. Those individuals or married couples who took the plunge found the ready support of those immigrants who had already flourished. There cannot be one established Cardi family unable to name a relative who had gone east.

The history of three families from Cardiganshire will suffice to demonstrate the family and inter-family connections and the way in which many of them returned to farming or, later, progressed to different professions.

First of all we examine the family of Anne Thomas, now of Watford. Her story reflects clearly the network of family connections within the milk trade in London. Her maternal grandparents, Josuah and Anne Davies were from Cryncoed, Derwen Gam. They had four children, David, Jack, Bess and Hetty and all of them established a successful milk business in London.

David married Gwladys Evans of Dihewid and then bought a milk business in Edmondton in Enfield, London. Later they returned to farming in Tregaron.

Jack married Sally Hopkins and bought a business in Kentish Town to the North West in Camden. One of their sons, Granville, returned to Cardiganshire to farm. Another

Edgar Morgan with an early version of a milk cart
(Anne Thomas)

Edgar Morgan with an early version of the milk cart (Anne Thomas)

son, Emlyn and his wife, Margaret Jones from Tregaron stayed on after his father's death to run a business with his mother in Shirland Road, Then he, too retired to Tregaron. A third son, Glyn became an electrician.

Hetty married and owned a dairy in Shepherds Bush to the south of the city and then another in Holloway to the north. She later retired to Swansea.

Bess, Anne's mother went to London to work for her future husband's aunt in Kensington in the city centre. She later opened her own business in Bromley by Bow, Tower Hamlets. After her marriage, she and her husband Dan Morgan moved to a milk business on the outskirts in Barking until the outbreak of the war.

Most of Anne's family moved to London partly because the initiative shown by two of her mother's sisters who had married and settled there. Her paternal grandmother, Elizabeth married David Morgan, originally from Brecon. He was killed in a coal mining accident and Elizabeth then moved to London where her son, Dan, who was Anne's father, had moved. His brothers and sisters had businesses in various London districts: Kensington, Kennington, Maida Vale and Holborn.

A second family worthy of our attention is that of Esgair-garn, Llanddewibrefi, another example of the migration of a large number of a family. Lewis (1864-1939) and Sarah Jane Lloyd (1864-1951) had sixteen children, four of whom died in infancy. To support the family, the father worked in the coalfields during the winter, From among the twelve surviving children, nine worked in the London milk trade, four of them returning to farm in Cardiganshire in later years. The history of four of the family illustrates the theme perfectly.

Daniel was first; he left in 1911. His terms of agreement are seen in a previous chapter.

A brother, Moses (Moss) followed in the 1920s to work initially with his brother Daniel and thus following the tradition of learning the trade from a relative. He married Laura Mary Jones from Llanberis and with his brother's help bought the lease of a shop in Islington.

One of the daughters of Esgair-garn was Mary, and she married Evan Edwards, who was himself one of twelve children and the descendant of a drover. After working in various occupations in Wales he left for London to start a business in Tufnell Park. Later, Evan and Mary had a business in Finsbury Park. They were there until they retired and returned to Tregaron. In the meantime they had helped Sam Jones, a neighbouring farmer back in Wales to undertake a business in Tufnell Park. This again was typical of the tradition of offering a helping hand. Later, Sam was joined by a brother who started a business in Peckham.

We come to yet a third family from Llanddewibrefi. The present connection is Helen Jones, Aberaeron. Her maternal grandfather, Thomas was the fifth child of Esgair-garn. Helen is also descended from another large Llanddewibrefi family, the Pant-y-blawd family. There, six of the ten children left for London. Jenno, the eldest being the first to leave. Then she and her husband Will took over a business in West London and after seven years they returned to Llanddewibrefi.

Jenno was followed to London by four brothers, Martin, Bert, Gordon and Tudor and they, in turn, by their sister Megan. She and her husband Elwyn ran a business in Chelsea. Gordon had a business in Drury Lane while Tudor ran a sandwich bar in Shaftsbury Avenue. Martin married a daughter of Thomas Lloyd of the Esgair-garn family. They were Helen's parents.

Gareth Davies today lives in Cardiff but his father, John, was from Capel Madog near Aberystwyth and was one of

J. Lewis Dairy and general shop,
with Catherine Davies and Jane Evans
(Anne Thomas)

David Davies' shop, with family group
(Anne Thomas)

eight children. John moved to London to work with his two brothers, William and Tom in their dairy in Harlesden. William moved to another shop in the north of the city. Gareth's mother was born in Taliesin and had left school at fourteen years of age. Two years later she went to London to work for a Welsh family who kept a shop in Brixton. She met her future husband in a dairy in Olympia and they were married in the Welsh chapel in Clapham in 1938. They continued with the business in Harlesden. Gareth remembers how his father started work every morning at four, ready to receive the milk delivery from a farm in Harrow. He used hand-carts and horse-drawn carts before turning to electrical floats and bottled milk. At the back of the shop were stables and a hay-loft, an echo of days gone by. They had a bottle-washing machine using boiling water and soda.

Another case was the family of Stephen Jones born in 1907 on Felinfach Farm, Talybont, Cardiganshire. The family moved to farm at Ynystudur, Tre'r Ddôl. There were seven children and the four girls of the family worked as maids at various farms. Their mother's sister lived in King's Cross and she persuaded three of the four girls in the family to go to London. Bessie, the eldest daughter married Jack Williams and kept a shop in Stratford Road, Kensington. The eldest son, John, and was entitled by tradition to inherit the farm; however he showed little interest in farming and decided when seventeen years old to go to London to work in his sister's shop. Meanwhile, another brother and sister left for London leaving behind only two of the seven.

Another Welsh family that ventured into the dairy business in London was that of Darren Fawr, Llandysul. Firstly, two brothers departed and founded a business near the Elephant and Castle. They were followed by a third brother who established a business in the East End. The fourth of the six children, Margaret married a Lampeter man in 1938. They inherited Margaret's aunt's business. On the outbreak of the war, the husband was called up leaving his wife to run the business. In another chapter we read how she lost everything during the bombing and forced to return to Wales.

As well as the exodus of whole families to London, we hear tell of couples going. An early example of a couple leaving their homeland to face the challenge of the big city was that of Edward and Mary Jones who left Talgarreg in 1870. In the local paper *Y Gambo* some twenty years ago, E. Lloyd Jones traced the family's story. Edward was one of the Henbant family and Mary originated from Pontrhydygroes. Edward went to work in David Evans' shop in Oxford Street, later having his own milk business in Highgate. He kept Welsh Black cattle for milking and as he was close to the Caledonian Market, he did a lot of business there. He kept in touch with his background in Wales. For years he sent a cask of beer to Henbant by train to Llandysul to celebrate the hay harvest. He died in London in 1927 and was buried in Highgate Cemetery where Karl Marx was laid to rest. Today, the old dairy serves as a warehouse to a Pakistani businessman and is storehouse and shop used to keep and sell imported goods.

As noted, succession was prominent among those who left for London. Gwilym Thomas Jenkins from Devil's Bridge, father of Gwenllian Jenkins of Llanfabon, Caerffili, represented the third generation to undertake dairying in the city. Evan Jenkins, Gwenllian's great grandfather was born in 1829. He was a lead miner who died when only 46 years old. His widow and two sons moved to London; she was described in the 1891 Census as the owner of a dairy in Clerkenwell. Their two sons, Thomas and John followed her into the milk trade. Thomas had a dairy in Bermondsey in 1881 and later in Newington and Battersea. In an obituary in the *Welsh Gazette* he was described as a poet of standing and a skilful 'englynwr' (an englyn being a stanza in the strict metre) who wrote under the bardic name of Didymus Gyfarllwyd winning eisteddfodic chairs in Wales and London.

The second son, John was a milkman throughout his working life from 1895 to 1949. He ran businesses in Battersea, Willesden and Southwark. He was one of the founders of Clapham Junction Chapel in 1895 and in his 80s travelled regularly to Griff's Welsh Bookshop in Charring Cross and to Westminster whenever the Welsh Questions sessions were held in the Chamber. His son Gwilym (Gwenllian's father) helped his own father in the Usk Road Dairy and loved telling her how he once saw Gwilym Lloyd George being bathed in a zinc bath when he was delivering milk to the Lloyd George family. One notable Welshman who used to call at her grandfather's shop was the poet Dewi Emrys. Some believed that Dewi was unpopular among his fellow Welsh in London but according to her grandfather, that was not so.

Gwenllian, like her father before her, rejoices in her Welsh roots. What is particularly interesting about the family is that their story not only outlines their business history over three generations, but also illustrates those literary and religious interests which they brought with them from Wales and sustained in a foreign environment. Another example is Owen Davies, a native of Llanarth, who had a Dairy in Tottenham, but he retained his interest in Welsh culture by having membership of the Gorsedd, adopting the bardic name Delynog.

My parents were exceptions from among those families that left Cardiganshire. Both were the youngest of large families.

Evan Edwards from Tregaron, a descendant of a drover who had 11 children.
He ran businesses, with his wife, in Tufnell Park and Finsbury Park.
(Evan Jones, Cardiff)

My mother outside their shop
in Clapham

John Stephen Jones, Ynys Tudur,
Tre'r-ddôl, c. 1930s
(Carys Bridden)

*Tom Lloyd, one of the
Esgair-garn family
(Helen Jones)*

*Jenno, an Esgair-garn daughter
with her husband, Wil and his
brother, Martin, outside their shop
(Helen Jones)*

*Gwenllian Jenkins' family dairy, Clerkenwell
(Gwenllian Jenkins)*

My father's association with the milk trade was remote; my mother was from Caerwedros on the coast and there the tradition was for the men to join the Merchant Navy but there was no corresponding outlet for a girl. My mother had to leave school at thirteen but she undertook courses in dairying and won a scholarship to study for a Diploma in that subject at Aberystwyth University. Even so, when my parents met, the attraction of London proved too strong. They joined the vast outflow and ran a number of businesses in Shoreditch, Brixton, Clapham and Richmond. I, however, had no desire to join the trade and I decided to pursue a career in the sciences. I never lost my respect towards for who possessed the persistence and determination necessary when joining the dairy trade.

The tradition, however, was maintained by other family members. My mother was followed to London by a cousin, Phoebe James from Brongest. She married, and she and her husband Jim Boudier kept a shop in Gray's Inn Road until well after the end of World War II.

A member of the Cilie family was again an exception but for a different reason. The tale is related by Jon Meirion

Phoebe and Jim Boudier outside their shop in Gray's Inn Road (Christine Boudier)

Jones in his book *Morwyr y Cilie* (The Sailors of Cilie). There he tells the story of his father, Jac Alun Jones, grandson of the head of the Cilie family. Captain Jac Alun was the son of Esther, one of the Cilie girls. He went to sea in 1924 on the *SS Ravenshaw*. However, the 30s depression

*Jac Alun, of the Cilie, Cwm Tydu family,
in Finsbury Park
(Jon Meirion Jones)*

resulted in the majority of Britain's ships and 1935, being laid off. Between 1933 a 1935, Captain Jac joined the milk trade in London keeping a shop in Finsbury Park. He gave a vivid account of his experiences in the English capital to his son:

I learnt a lot about how our families fared in the big city with your mother Ellena saying that if the members of Capel y Wig knew how people behaved here!

When the depression was at its height, families bought a penny's worth of tea, margarine, biscuits and milk at a time. This was a very constrained life. Rising at 4.30 in the morning, weekdays, Sundays and bank holidays. But I had Sunday free so I could attend the service in King's Cross where the incomparable Elfed was the minister. Following the service, I would go for supper to Lyons Corner House and thence to Hyde Park to hear the speakers in full flow. The hunger marchers from Jarrow, Birmingham and Harrow would gather there. I remember the Welsh miners singing hymns. Rows of people cast their rare pennies like manna on the street ahead of them.

It was a strange time. A pint of milk was three and a half pence and half a pint was a penny three farthings. This was the first and last time that I would deal in fractions. We never made a fortune, but I was glad to see the end of the great adventure and return to the tranquillity of the countryside.

But seafaring was the chosen career of the Cilie grandson, and after eighteen months that seemed, he said, like a five-year prison sentence, he joined the Pengreep as second mate and in time attaining his captaincy but even so writing poetry in the tradition of his Cilie ancestors.

Whereas most London Welsh milk traders hailed from Cardiganshire or North Carmarthenshire, there were exiles from other parts of Wales as well. Yet, even among such backgrounds we are able to discover Cardiganshire connections. Nancy Roberts from Tregarth, Bangor with her daughter Jois and son in law Richard Snelson, now living in Denbigh, detail a family originally from Pontrhydfendigaid.

Evan Jones was born in Lledrod in 1841, and he and his wife Margaret had eight children. Four of them, three brothers and a sister left for London to run The People's Dairy in Lambeth Walk. Later, during the Great War they moved to the Hampshire Farm Dairy in Barkworth Road where they worked three milk rounds under the name Jones Brothers. The business ended in 1957 upon the death of the sister, Maggie.

Meanwhile Ann, the oldest of Evan and Margaret's eight children left with her husband, Thomas Davies of Pontrhydfendigaid, for Penrhiwceiber to work in the coalfields. They, in turn, had eight children and one of them, Margaret married a North Wales man Ted Hughes (b. 1896). His father was a miller from Glasinfryn near Bangor. Ted had worked as a quarryman in Bethesda but left for the 'South' to find work. He later moved back to Mynydd Llandegai where Nancy was born in 1923. Margaret's youngest brother, David moved north to live with them. They then decided to try to find a better life in London and opened a shop and dairy in Combermere Road, Stockwell The shop is now a dwelling. Later they moved across the river to Garth Dairy in Bramley Road, North Kensington with David still living with them. Margaret died in 1943 but Ted stayed in business moving next door to keep the Badge Café in 1950. In the mid 1960s, many of the streets in the neighbourhood were demolished and today both the shop and café are beneath the concrete pillars of the Westway. Margaret and Ted were buried in Bangor.

When the family was at Bramley Road and Barkworth Road, relatives from Penrhiwceiber visited them and Margaret's brother, Dick worked in the business at the latter premises. Dick married Sarah Jane Lloyd, one of the Esgairgarn, Llanddewibrefi family referred to earlier in this chapter and they ran a business in Latimer Road.

The history of the Jones family from Lledrod follows a common pattern in the history of the Welsh in London. Beginning in Cardiganshire, the story moves to other parts of Wales in the search for work in the heavy industries such as coal and slate, both industries flourishing in Wales at the time. Ultimately, however, it was the Cardiganshire goal of finding a better life that won out with the families moving to London to develop their milk businesses before being forced, after World War II, to diversify after the smaller milk businesses were swallowed by the large conglomerates. They eventually returned to Wales to be buried and, ironically, the sites of their previous labours are also now buried beneath the concrete as their adopted city continued to grow and develop.

There are other exceptions worth noting. John Jacob (1897-1979) was a miner from the Rhondda, He was injured in the mine and although he retrained to work as an engineer, he was unable to find suitable work during the 1933 depression. And so he emigrated. He joined his brother in law Tom Jones and marketed under the name 'Jones and Jacob'. Tom later returned to Wales but John

John Jacob, the collier milkman
(Peggy Beaven)

Jacob remained, an example of a dairyman who wasn't from an agricultural background.

There are also representatives of families north of Cardiganshire. Margaret Humphrey's family hales from Montgomeryshire. Her Grandfather, John Jones, (1863-1951), went from Uwchgarreg, Machynlleth, when 14, towork in a dairy and in 1898 married Margaret Evans from Llanwrtyd Wells, already working with a Welsh family. They had six children of whom, Margaret's mother was the eldest. She, with her brother, went to work at relative's business in Notting Hill but later married William Evans who already had a dairy in Highbury. The family later followed the pattern of returning to their home area, in this case, in the forties.

Others represented the north during this period. William Davies left Tywyn for London early in the twentieth century. His Welsh was limited but like most other Welsh immigrants, he succeeded.

Another family with no direct connection with Cardiganshire were Rees and Catherine Price from Llangammarch, now in Powys. Annabelle Thomas, their great niece, relates how they went to London with a young family in 1886. They traded first from Shepherds Bush but later had several branches of their business scattered throughout London, known as the Rees Price Dairies and reputed at one stage to be the largest one-man owned dairy business in London. One of the daughters, born in Wales before they went, is remembered as singing a nursery rhyme before she went – and which many in Wales learnt at the time and later:

Fe af i Llundain glamai,
Os byddaf byw ac iach,
Arhosa' i ddim yng Nghymru,
I dorri 'nghalon fach.
Mae arian mawr yn Llundain
A swper gyda'r nos,
A mynd i'r gwely'n gynnar
A chodi am chwech o'r gloch.

I'll go to London on Mayday
Should I have strength and health,
I'll not tarry more here in Wales
Where I will break my heart.
There's wealth galore in London
And supper every night,
And early nights a sleeping
And rising at six o'clock.

The words are an interesting expression of the expectations of those planning to make the journey.

Some left Wales later in the century. Eluned Jones left Maesteg for Tottenham in 1947. John Richard Jones' family hailed from Powys. His father left for London, yet another example of a non-Cardi immigrant although his wife was a Cardi from Nebo. They left for London like many before them and after them because of the dearth of opportunity in Wales. They were married in 1939 in Shirland Road chapel. John spent the war years in relative safety back in Wales and can recall earning pocket money by helping his father on the milk round. He must have been one of the youngest to walk the milky way.

Although there were exceptions, it is clear that most of those who emigrated to the London milk trade were from large or poor families – or both – from Cardiganshire. It is worth noting that despite the more affluent life the city had to offer, 'home' was always Wales. And the chosen calling that so many exiles returned to when the need or the opportunity arose, was farming. The story of Maldwyn Pugh's family, Jack and Betty Pugh and their daughter Jean, encapsulates both the need to go to London for employment and also the nature of the work in the milk trade as described in this and the previous chapter. It is worth relating in Maldwyn's own words:

'Jack hailed from Llanidloes and Betty from Aberaeron; both went to London to seek employment, met, married and after a spell in a Balham Dairy, took over Oxford Express Dairy in Frith Street, Soho, in 1934.

The property was owned by the Townsend Estate. The shop sold milk, cheese , ham, bacon and the usual groceries. After the war it sold filled rolls and sandwiches. It opened at 8am and closed at 6pm Monday to Friday, 8am to 1pm on Saturday and for 1 hour on a Sunday to sell perishable goods only.

Supplies were bought from wholesalers; the milk from the London Wholesale Dairies and Independent Milk Suppliers, L.W.D. and I.M.S.. The companies operated differently, in that the L.W.D. made only one delivery, in the early morning. I.M.S. had a crew going around in their own truck to see if anyone needed more supplies later in the day.

Prior to the Second World War, and for a brief period after it, all milk was supplied in churns and had to be bottled. The bottles were usually owned and identified with the dairy name on them. These were wide necked bottles which were sealed with cardboard tops which also identified the dairy. These bottles had to be washed and refilled on a daily basis, usually by the milkmen. They normally started work about 6am and finished around lunchtime, 7 days a week. One of the milkmen had a second job, scene shifting in the local theatre.

Later, milk was supplied already bottled by the wholesalers. Churns were either 5 or 10 gallons. The milk orders were done on a daily basis and had to be in at the wholesalers by 4pm for delivery the next morning, usually 3-4 am. The milk was left outside the premises, either outside on the pavement or outside the lock-up from where the milkmen worked.

The shop had a number of milk rounds, delivering milk to flats, restaurants, cafes and houses in the area. The milk was generally carted around on milk barrows, three wheeled monstrosities made mainly of wood. The milkmen employed in Frith Street were all veterans of the First World War. One of these did his deliveries on a trike, a three wheeled cycle with a load area at the front and the rear wheel framework pivoting about a fulcrum point under that. That particular milkman had lost his left arm but was very adept at loading and unloading the milk, rolling 'his own' one handed, and keeping his books.

Betty Pugh died in the late 1970's. The business was then operated by Jack Pugh, daughter Jean and younger son Islwyn. It finally closed on Jack's death in 1985 and was probably the last Welsh dairy in the Soho area.

The photo on page 60 shows the family on the last day of trading. Jean retired to Aberaeron and died in 2010. Maldwyn, Jack and Betty's second son did not enter the milk trade but qualified as a mechanical engineer.

He also describes how the dairy was very much the meeting place for visitors from Aberaeron and Llanidloes as was the case for other such establishments for visitors from respective home villages.

Most left to make a better living than that which was possible in Cardiganshire at the beginning of the twentieth century but they would not necessarily realize the wealth that lay in the imagination of those who remained. Nevertheless, in is worth noting some notable successes.

For example, Jo Pleshakov, currently living in Vancouver, takes great pride in her great grandfather, Richard Williams's story. He left Corris, now in Gwynedd, around 1845 where he had been a quarryman. He married Catherine Jones, also from Corris, in Jewin Chapel. The 1851 census records him as a stonemason but by 1871 he is a cow keeper in Blackfriars; then in 1881 is described as a dairyman. By 1891 he is listed as a 'milk contractor' in Hornsey and by the 1901 he is a retired dairyman living in Islington. Obituaries of his death speak of him as a highly regarded member of the Charing Cross Road Calvinistic Chapel. His son, Howell Jones Williams, later Sir Howell, was equally prominent in London Welsh circles and is credited with donating the land on which the London

Welsh Centre was built in Gray's Inn Road. Might we surmise that it was acquaintance with Cardiganshire milkmen that led Richard Williams to follow their tradition? He and his son certainly displayed the chapel loyalties and philanthropic contributions to Welsh causes that were characteristic of the London Welsh.

Another is Dewi Morgan, who left Bethania for London as a seventeen year-old youth with just two pound notes and a one-way ticket to Paddington in his pocket to work as a milkman. He exhibited the characteristic thrift of his race by investing ten shillings (50 pence) per week from his wages. During World War II he managed to buy a number of businesses that he developed and sold on to conglomerates. Having bought and sold numerous businesses, he and his wife Nanno returned to Pencarreg Farm, Llanrhystud, in January 1963 before retiring in 1981 and moving to Pennant. His success resulted in his financial support for numerous good causes in his home county including renovating the local Trefilan Church to financing specialist equipment for cardiac treatment at Bronglais Hospital, Aberystwyth.

There is a lengthy history of the 'exile's patronage' involving supporting relatives and deserving causes in the old neighbourhood. This was typical of the great majority of the exiles. Roger Davies' family are farmers today in Llanwrtyd Wells. His grandfather's brother left for the London milk trade early in the nineteenth century. Following his success he financed the purchase of a new house and a smithy for his nephew, a blacksmith. He contributed substantially as well towards the wellbeing of other members of his family and towards building a new chapel in the area. Roger's father was the youngest of thirteen children; some followed their grandfather to London and they, in turn, contributed financially to relatives back in Wales.

There are other examples of famous exiles that did likewise. Sir David James left Pantyfedwen above Strata Florida to help his relatives run a dairy in Westminster. He expanded into the grain trade and in the 1930s diversified into the world of entertainment. He owned thirteen cinemas including the first-ever multi-screen arena to open in London, the Palladium in Palmer's Green in 1920. His name still lives, particularly in the field of the eisteddfodau held annually at Pontrhydfendigaid, Cardigan and Lampeter. At Pontrhydfendigaid, where he grew up, he financed the building of a 3,000 seat pavilion, a playing field, a community centre, a village hall and a library. He also paid for the stained glass windows seen at St Mary's Church, Strata Florida through the Pantyfedwen Trust, a charity which also finances the upkeep of the cemetery where he lies.

Another who became a great business success was Alban Davies of Llanrhystud. Following his marriage he went to London to work in his brother -in-law's dairy before buying the Hitchman Dairies. By the 1920s he was employing a staff of 500 and producing 120,000 gallons of milk daily. Following a visit to America he returned with the idea of replacing the cardboard milk bottle tops with metal caps.

Alban Davies was a member of Walthamstow Council for nine years. He founded Moriah Welsh Chapel in the borough and according to T.I. Ellis in 'Crwydro Llundain' he would contribute one tenth of his earnings annually to the cause. He returned to live at Brynawel, Llanrhystud, was a County Councillor and in 1940 was appointed High Sheriff. He founded the Deva old people's home in Aberystwyth. He bought three hundred acres of land on Penglais Hill and presented it to the University College of Wales Aberystwyth to ensure that no-one else could develop the site. Most of the University Campus is today located on that site. Alban Davies died in 1951.

Another example is Evan Evans, who left Llangeitho at the end of the nineteenth century with a one-way ticket to London bought for him by a relative who had offered him work in London but with the cooperation of a network of London Welsh acquaintances he managed to profit from the opportunities available in the capital at the time and joined the milk trade. His mother's influence and emphasis on family allegiance led him to support two of his relatives and help them to set up their own businesses.

He developed his own tourist business, ferrying visitors by horse and cart and then by charabanc and bus. He bought the Celtic Hotel in Russell Square. He was described by T. I. Ellis as 'the Thomas Cook of Wales'. So progressive was Evan Evans in his ideas that the following notice appeared in number 33 of *Y Ddolen*, the London Welsh newspaper in 1933:

An aeroplane will leave London at 8am, Aug 30, for the Llangeitho Show. Lunch will be provided. Fare £5.

When Jewin Chapel had to be rebuilt after the war (it was damaged by a bomb in 1940), Evan Evans contributed substantially towards the cost. Such was his influence and status that he was elected Mayor of St Pancras twice, before and during the war and was admitted to the exclusive Loriners' Guild. Although the Guild originally had business connotations, its purpose by now was humanitarian and social; membership reflected a social status of note. Evan Evans died in 1965 when he was 83 years old.

One who was a member of the Loriners' Guild much earlier was John Morgan, born in Aberystwyth in 1822. He left to run a milk business in Clerkenwell, describing himself as 'John Morgan Gentleman and in possession of property in London and Llanfihangel Genau'r Glyn'. He died in 1893.

Another Cardi who, like Evan Evans became mayor of St
Pancras was Sir David Davies. He was born the son of a
farmer in Ty'n Cae, Y Berth near Tregaron in 1870. He left
London to join the milk trade and was appointed the first
leader of the London Milk Retailers' Association. He was
Mayor of his borough from 1912 to 1922. He was elected
Conservative MP and was a member and Alderman on
London City Council. His wife, Mary Anne Edwards was
from Eglwysfach.

We have examples of the drive philanthropy of some
London dairymen who were from outside Cardiganshire.
William Price (1865-1938) was born in Llanwrtyd Wells,
son of a farmer and the sixth of nine children. He began by
opening a retail dairy in West London and then became a
partner in the Great Western and Metropolitan Dairies
before setting up United Dairies. Through the business he
was responsible for ensuring a regular supply of milk in
London throughout the Great War and during the 1926
General Strike. His contribution to London's civic and
religious life was just as notable; he became a JP, a deacon in
his Presbyterian chapel as well as being a patron for the
family chapel at Llanwrtyd Wells. He was knighted in 1922.

It is worth noting that the United Dairies' Secretary was
the Welsh-speaking Welshman from Holywell, D. R.
Hughes (1874-1953). For many years he was editor of the
staff magazine and joint editor of *Y Ddolen*, the London
Welsh newspaper.

Some of those who thronged to London from Wales
created much wealth. But they were ready to work hard and
to share their riches as well. There was a readiness to
support their fellow Welsh who followed them to London
while not forgetting the good causes back home that were
close to their heart. As poet Ceri Wyn said in a couplet:

Sarah Jones' gravestone,
Llanfihangel Genau'r Glyn
(Bethan and Richard Hartnup)

200 SING HYMNS AT STATION

Woman Who Was Loved In The East End

TWO hundred people took part in hymn-singing at Euston Station when the body of Mrs. Sarah Jones, an East End dairywoman, was sent back to her native Wales for burial to-day.

Mrs. Jones, who was 56, was loved by all in the East End.

Her Generosity

No one who asked her for assistance was refused.

If, on her round, she heard of a case of sickness among the poor, she would give them eggs and other provisions from her shop, and sometimes complete strangers were invited in to have a meal with the family.

Many Wreaths

She had 11 children—seven sons and four daughters.

After a service at the house the procession left the shop in Stony-lane, Middlesex-street, where she had lived for 36 years.

The funeral cars used were covered with scores of wreaths and bunches of flowers.

Sarah Jones' funeral report

Nid yw dwrn y Cardi'n dynn
Â'i gyfoeth pan fo'r gofyn.

The Cardi's fist is never tight
He shares his wealth when needed.

The aim was to work hard, succeeding and returning to Wales with clear evidence of that success. And when a Welsh exile died amidst his labours he would, almost inevitably, be taken back home to be buried in the family plot. Following the late Sunday service the coffin would be ferried to Platform 1 at Paddington Station and then taken by train to the nearest station to the deceased's home. The congregation would have joined the family mourners on the platform and as the train slowly departed, the precentor would hit the opening notes of David Charles of Carmarthen's hymn: 'O Fryniau Caersalem' (From the Hills of Jerusalem).

We have a good example of such a ceremony after Sarah Jones of Stoney Lane, Middlesex Road in the East End died in 1937. Such events were so special that they would be noted in the local London newspapers. Sarah's departure attracted two hundred mourners to Euston Station

(Paddington was the usual station) to bid her farewell. The 59 year old exile was described in *The Star* as one who had been kind to those in need. She distributed eggs and other various goods from her shop free of charge among the sick and other unfortunates in the area. She was said to welcome strangers to share meals around the family table. She and her husband Henry had eleven children, seven of them girls.

A funeral service was held at the family home, where she had lived for 36 years. It was reported that the motorcade of three dozen cars following the hearse was decked with flowers and wreaths and that mourners thronged the streets. Hymns were sung on the station platform. She was interned, like her husband and their baby before, at Llanfihangel Genau'r Glyn Church cemetery. At the base of her gravestone and beneath her name is written:

Hyn a allodd hon, hi â'i gwnaeth

That which she could, she did.

People's Dairy, Lambeth Walk
(Richard and Jois Snelson)

Jones Bros, Barkworth Road
(Richard and Jois Snelson)

Ted Hughes, Bramley Road
(Richard and Jois Snelson)

Roundsmen and barrows outside Owen Davies' Dairy, Tottenham
(Christine Boudier)

Fact and Fiction

Shortly before Christmas 1996, S4C presented a drama series called 'Y Palmant Aur' (The Golden Pavement). This was a story of a family that had been part of the milk trade during the last century. The essence of the story was the contrast between two major characters, one of whom stayed at home in Cardiganshire and the other who had gone to London. So we find Ifan at home, farming Ffynnon Oer and Isaac, who has been successful selling milk in the English capital.

The story filmed by the television company Opus, opens with the death of the matriarch of the family and the birth of an illegitimate child. The film was based on detailed research of contemporary periodicals and the interviewing of those who had experienced life in the milk trade in London. The authoress of the story that ran for four series was Manon Rhys. She also published the story in three novels, *Siglo'r Crud* (Rocking the Cradle), *Rhannu'r Gwely* (Sharing the Bed) and *Cwilt Rhacs* (A Rag Quilt). She wrote from personal experience after members of both sides of her family had been part of the London milk trade. Although she was born in the Rhondda, her mother hailed from Ffos-y-ffin and her father from Tregaron.

The basic message of the story – true to a large extent – was that it was possible to do well in London but that staying at home on the farm was hard labour. That theme threads through the whole drama.

Ffynnon Oer represented a traditional smallholding in Cardiganshire during the 1920s. There, the tenant had to struggle with poor acidic soil that needed careful and consistent tending to provide any kind of living. That was the kind of smallholding where Kitchener Davies, the authoress' father had been raised, Llain, bordering Tregaron

'Y Palmant Aur' cast, the tv drama series that accurately depicted the story
(S4C)

Bog near Llwynpiod. In 'Y Palmant Aur' it is implied that any alternative way of life, especially one as romantic as that in London, was certain to be economically superior.

The smallholder's life in Cardiganshire entailed hard work for little return. It is this that led to the unfair description of the Cardi as being exceptionally parsimonious. This undoubtedly contributed to the incomer's monetary success but there was also the preparedness to cooperate and a willingness to lend a helping hand.

It might be expected that simple folk like these, having come from the wildernesses of the countryside would have succumbed to the bright lights and temptations of the city. There are tales of newcomers from the rural areas of Cardiganshire being taken to the greyhound races at the White City to warn them against the temptations. How easy it would be to risk hard-earned money on a greyhound, something that led to the saying, 'Going to the dogs'. How often was the warning given to keep to the straight and narrow?

'Y Palmant Aur' was fictional. But it could have been true. Manon Rhys drew from her many experiences and recollections. Below you will read the reminiscences of an exceptional woman, who personally experienced this kind of life. She is Ann Jones from Bronnant. These are her recollections; they speak for themselves:

Ann Jones, Bronnant
(Megan Hayes)

I left my home at Pantddafad, Bronnant when I was twelve years old in 1933 with my parents and my brother Dan. It was a smallholding and my granny lived there, a smallholding where I live now. The reason why my parents decided to pack up their bags was poverty. The soil was poor and life was hard. Mother worked as a seamstress just to bring in some extra pence. We had to leave or starve. I remember my father selling a calf for seven shillings and six pence. After feeding it with milk for a week, the purchaser could sell it for four or five times as much. Mind you, seven shillings and six pence was a lot of money in those days. In order to make ends meet, mother worked at sewing for three pence a day.

Pantddafad, where we lived, was only 54 acres and we kept a cow and calf, a pig and a few hens. Later some of the land was sold leaving us only seventeen acres. After grandma left for Arfron, where I now live, I would sit with her on the little settle where she would read me *Y Drysorfa Fach* (The Small Treasury) by candlelight, the candle grease dripping over her clothes. I had to repeat after her and that was how I learnt to read.

We left for London on the train from Tregaron Station with the furniture following in a Pickfords' lorry. I wasn't sorry to leave. For a twelve-year old girl it was a great adventure. My parents had bought a milk vending business in Central Street, Hoxton in the Borough of Hackney in the East End. The business was close to the large City banks. A relative of my mother was a house agent in London and it was he who found them the business. My brother and I attended the local school in Hoxton amongst all the Cockneys. It was rather a rough school but we got on well there without any serious problems.

Then the business next door to the dairy came on the market, a Jewish shop. My father bought it and turned it into a bar selling snacks such as sandwiches, rolls, coffee and tea. Because of its proximity to the City where the banks and big money were situated, we were very busy.

My brother and I soon acclimatised to life in the big city. I had little English; at least I could say 'Good morning', 'Good afternoon' and 'Thank you very much'. My father spoke good English but my mother wasn't as fluent. She described her English as 'a tramp's English'.

My brother Dan did not join the business. He chose to go to the field of medicine. He was admitted to Barts Hospital Medical School where he pursued optical studies. He graduated as an optician and then as an eye specialist. He went to Harley Street and was appointed as the eye specialist for the prisoners at Wormwood Scrubs Prison. He attended there three mornings a week.

Having settled in London our visits to Bronnant

were few and far between. The fact is that we were too busy to go. The business needed our constant attention and there was no time for holidays.

We didn't leave even during the war. We managed to survive that nightmare. Many buildings around us were bombed. When the siren sounded, we would shelter in the cellars of a large old brewery nearby. Even then, during one raid by the Luftwaffe, a hundred were killed there; I remember bodies lying around everywhere.

My father, Morgan Ifor Morgan had his own milk round. Between the dairy and food bar, we employed two local girls. Then dad decided to look for a laundrette. He found one in Chiswick in an area of large, fashionable houses inhabited by many stage stars like Tommy Cooper. Dad thought that such a business would suit him after retiring from the dairy round. There again, business was good. After all, the gentry of Chiswick were not prepared to wash their clothes in a tub as mother had done back in Pantddafad. They preferred to use a washing machine. The laundrette doors closed and locked automatically every night. Therefore if you were not out by nine, you were there till morning. This too was a successful undertaking.

There was much business acumen in the family. R. O. Williams' sister was my father's mother, that is, my grandmother. R. O. Williams was one of Tregaron's foremost businessmen.

My father then bought a business in Harlesden. This was a self-service store. The shop was situated in the middle of a very busy area. Nearby was the Walls factory and dozens of the workers called by constantly.

The exiled Cardis met regularly in chapel on a Sunday and especially in the meeting after the service over a cup of tea in the vestry. In Jewin where we were members, we took turns to prepare the tea. There, everyone would be caught up in the weekly news about the old home. The minister was the Rev. D. S. Owen. I attended the services fairly regularly, but not every Sunday; my brother and I had one Sunday a month free.

On those Sundays when we didn't attend Jewin, my brother and I travelled on a double-decker bus around London. We bought a day ticket for six pence. Mother prepared a box of food for us. We were in our element. It was the perfect way to get to get to know the city.

I remember all the activities associated with Jewin. I recall competing in various eisteddfodau. My father taught me to recite. I recited on the stage at Shoreditch Town Hall and won as well. Every Sunday night, concerts were held at the Welsh Centre in Grays Inn Road. Then it would be a meal in Lyons Corner House, one of the most popular eating venues among the London Welsh community. Two meals cost ten shillings. One could eat a bellyful of lunch. I remember Dick, mother's brother saying that he and his cousin, Tom Penlan, ate a whole duck each there. The size of their bellies betrayed their massive appetites!

My father loved singing and he was an exceptional singer. He had been the precentor back in Bronnant. He was one of the Navy Hall children. He loved acting and appeared in plays directed by the minister, D. S. Owen. They were Welsh plays, of course. D. S. Owen was married to the daughter of Willie Evans who kept a shop and small café in St John's Street.

I remember a large congregation frequenting Jewin. Among them was Evan Evans, owner of the Celtic Hotel in Russell Square. He also ran a fleet of buses. He was Mayor of St Pancras twice during the war. Nans, his wife, was related to our family. Their son, Dafydd Gwyn

married Rhiannon who keeps the famous shop of the
same name at Tregaron. The shop, by the way, is
established in the old Emporium owned by the R. O.
Williams I referred to earlier.

I worked with my parents until I married. My
husband Tom was a farmer from Penuwch. He, too
moved to London following our wedding at Jewin. We
bought a shop in Stoke Newington between Islington
and Hackney. There we sold a variety of goods including
milk, of course; we had a local round. The venture was a
great success. Like my father we had a cart, or barrow. It
did not display the family name, only the business
address, 102 Matthias Road, Stoke Newington E. My
parents' milk business was at 129 Central Street.

Dick, my mother's brother worked for the
Independent Milk Supplies. He would carry the milk in
large cans in his pony and trap to the City. One day he
was delivering to a café as children played around his
pony and trap. And tragically, the pony dragged the trap
over a little girl and killed her. Dick was never the same
after that. Ever after, he suffered with a terrible stammer.

Despite the influence of Jewin, the shop would open
on Sundays but would close early at 1.00. In my parents'
case the shop would open at 7.00 am. It would remain
open till 6.00 pm. Tom and I would follow much the
same pattern, opening at 7.00 am and remaining open
for twelve hours. On Sundays we would open at 9.00 am
and close at noon. We would reserve Sunday afternoons
for accounting and stock-taking.

My favourite day was Thursday. I would finish
checking through the orders by around 1.00 pm. Then I
would make for Oxford Street and its shops such as D.H.
Evans and Selfriges. I would walk down Tottenham
Court Road and then up to Marble Arch. There I would

cross over and double back to Tottenham Court Road once more. I would then meet up with Tom at Lyons Corner House at 8.00 pm and we would pay half a crown for a taxi home. Being and living in London was cheap in those days.

I never wanted to leave London. But as a result of the rebuilding following the chaos caused by the blitz, our shop was possessed through a compulsory order and we returned to Bronnant in 1972 after spending fifty happy years in London. When I heard of the compulsory order I broke my heart. I cried for a month.

At least we arrived home from London alive and well. I witnessed many leaving London for home in coffins to be buried. For the majority, especially the older exiles, this was their wish. A train would leave Paddington's Platform 1 at 9.00 pm, the last train out. The coffin would be lying in the last carriage, the guard's van. The carriage doors would be left open so that the mourners could show their last respects before the train pulled out in a cloud of smoke. Then the mourners would sing one of the old hymns, 'O Fryniau Caersalem' (From the Hills of Jerusalem) or 'Mae nghyfeillion adre'n myned' (My friends are returning home'). These were suitable words as the dear departed was, indeed, returning home. Home was Cardiganshire.

Yes, I spent a happy half-century in London and would return tomorrow if my husband Tom and I were still together. Yes, I would return tomorrow.

Ann Jones' recollections were recorded for my research. Her memories were so vivid that I decided to include them word for word. I felt that her descriptions of her experiences in London incorporated all aspects of life in the dairy trade – a family fleeing from the hardship of the smallholding, the initial linguistic difficulties, the hard work, the importance of the chapel and the Welsh social life and the need to diversify; and, finally, having to sell their business and livelihood because of compulsory purchase orders. Truly, it can be claimed that Ann Jones' experiences are at the heart of this volume.

Religion, Culture and Recreation

We are in the vestry of Aberaeron's Tabernacle Chapel on the occasion of the town's annual exhibition. Amongst the visitors are two middle-aged men. They realise that they were fellow Welshmen from London. They chat, exchanging reminiscences. Then one says to the other:

I went to Clapham Junction. Where did you go?

The other the other realises the significance of the question and replies by naming another Welsh chapel in London. Any conversations between people who have London connections will surely soon turn to talk of chapel or church, and that without any encouragement.

An occurrence such as above crystallises the influence of the chapel – or to a lesser extent the church – had on London Welsh life when the milk trade was at its height. The situation was unique. Infrequently, if ever, would such a dialogue arise within any other group of people. Membership of a chapel or church was essential. Every denomination was represented in the capital just as in any village or town in Wales and as far as possible, the immigrants remained loyal to the sect they frequented in Wales. An application for membership would be forwarded to the appropriate place of worship as soon as the exile left Wales.

In June, 1912, the report by *The Welsh National Bazaar in Aid of London C. M. Churches* was published. The Bazaar was organised as a kind of joint marketing venture to bring the Welsh places of worship in the city together and to cooperate. One of the main stimulants of the venture was Margaret, wife of Lloyd George, Chancellor of the Treasury at the time.

In the publication *The Welsh in London 1400-2000* edited by Professor Emrys Jones, Rhidian Griffiths refers to a part of the report. It states that the Welsh places of worship had been established in order to provide services in Welsh for the many who were strangers to English:

Predominantly they are religious establishments and what they accomplish in this field is immeasurable. But nowadays, as well as their religious duties, the churches do immense work for the benefit of social and national wellbeing. They present a young man or woman who arrives in London from Wales something more than a shadow of their homes because they are creating the kind of society that is, from the point of view of life standards and behaviour in society, not unlike the village life in Wales by creating a connection with earlier life and conditions which make it difficult for the young to rush headlong into the dangers rife in the big cities. The main mission of the Welsh churches in London is to defend the moral character and deepen the spiritual experience of the hundreds of young people entrusted into their care, year after year by the parents of Wales. This trust, which involved much work, sacrifice and love was given voluntarily and was never betrayed.

Attending a place of worship brought back memories of the life that had been left behind in Wales, the fount of their culture and the barricade against the pangs of 'hiraeth'. It could be argued that the church or chapel ultimately satisfied the need amongst the exiles for certainty, and a compensation for the loss of the society that they had left behind.

Hard work was central to the Calvinistic philosophy but on a Sunday only the best clothes were worn. In his book *Y*

Ddinas Gadarn: Hanes Capel Jewin (The Strong City: The Story of Jewin Chapel) Gomer M. Roberts includes a letter written by a minister, Robert Hughes, in 1830 describing his impressions of Jewin's worshippers:

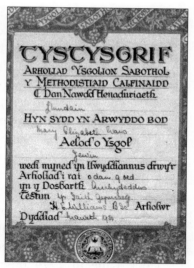

Sunday School exam certificate
(Mary Bott)

A congregation of gentlefolk ... But one caught my attention above all others, a man of gentlemanly appearance, about 45, sitting behind the clock in the front of the gallery. I thought he must of the East India Company; but I greatly disappointed when I went to the Cambrian, to the Sunday School, who did I see in the centre of the city, with a blue apron to his knees and a pitcher of milk in his hand, knocking on doors and shouting 'Milk' but in imagination, the great gentleman I had seen before.

Jewin was the oldest and the best known Methodist church. The congregation there was described by Professor Dafydd Jenkins and quoted thus by T. I. Ellis:

Milk people, almost invariably Cardis.

At their height, London's Welsh chapels could boast some of the nation's most charismatic preachers. Between 1904 and 1930, the minister at the Tabernacle, King's Cross was the Rev H. Elvet Lewis (Elfed) the hymnist, and Wales'

Archdruid from 1904 to 1908. Again, according to Dafydd Jenkins, it was almost a competition between the various chapels as they attempted to attract the cream of the Welsh society to their precincts. When Richard Owen was inducted minister to Holloway Chapel in 1887, there were three Welsh MPs present, T. E. Ellis, Thomas Lewis and Mabon. A prominent member of Shirland Road Methodist Chapel which opened in 1871 was William Price, previously referred to, who had been prominent in the campaign to build the chapel.

The London Branch of the Welsh Family History Society has done valuable work in chronicling the history of the Welsh chapels and churches in London. The sites of the places of worship have been recorded from the earliest in Cock Lane in 1774 onwards and include those closed, united or re-sited. Altogether, between various periods of existence, some 24 Calvinistic sites, six Wesleyan Methodist, 13 Independent, two Baptist chapels, six Anglican Churches and two international churches were recorded as being Welsh religious establishments in London.

An important task was the recording of the baptisms held in Jewin between 1838 and 1939. The records, as was the custom of the time, contained the names of baptised children and their parents and every father's address and work. One is immediately struck by the number of milkmen and cattle-keepers.

The statistics relative to baptisms can be expressed graphically, and so doing one can draw some very interesting sociological conclusions. The reason for the continuing low and even level of dairy people's children's baptisms between 1837-1851 can be attributed to the imposition of Elias' Law. According to Gomer M. Roberts in his history of Jewin, many of the worshipers feared for

Jewin Chapel Saint David's Day dinner, 1950s
(Andrew Jones)

Shoreditch Eisteddfod Programme (Margaret Jenkins)

Sunday observance and a campaign was therefore initiated to return to the Sabbath its original sanctity. John Elias, a prominent member of the Calvinistic clergy, decreed that children whose parents had besmirched the sanctity of the Sabbath by working on that day would not be allowed to be baptised in chapel. This Law was passed in 1835. Because the dairymen had no option but to work on Sundays, they had to go to chapels that were still prepared to baptise their children; it is not clear which chapels these were. It can be accepted that this law had been loosened after 1851 when one sees that the number of dairymen's children who were baptised had now increased substantially.

Between 1911 and 1920, there was a sudden decline in the number of dairymen's children who were baptised. This period, of course, includes World War I and the decline therefore can be attributed to the number of dairymen who enlisted from 1914 onwards. This is confirmed by the fact that many women from Wales left for London to help their families in their milk businesses. This trend was echoed during World War II.

There are two maxima in the statistics that record the annual baptisms – the turn of the nineteenth and the twentieth centuries and later, the thirties of the twentieth century. These can be attributed to the general slump in work opportunities for the Welsh back home and an upturn in the milk trade in London. That was when rural unemployment was at its worst as young people were compelled to seek alternative work to agriculture or rural crafts by following, possibly, relatives already established in dairy work.

As the second flood of incomers to London increased, so did the membership of the city's chapels. This is dramatically reflected in the membership records of Tabernacle Chapel in King's Cross. It was at its highest

Jewin Chapel Drama Group
(Ifor Evans)

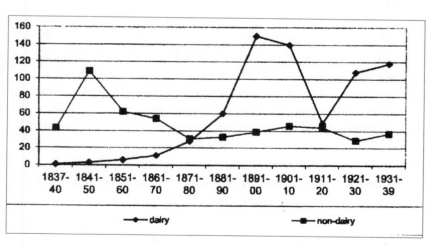

Jewin Baptism Graphs, 1838–1938
(LW Family History Association)

during the 1925-1938 reaching almost one thousand. At this time it was necessary to arrive early to ensure a seat for the 6.30 pm service. Afterwards, one sees a steady decline during the second half of the twentieth century (280 in 1970) leading to eventual closure early in the twenty-first century.

Sunday Morning services might have provided a dilemma among dairymen and their families, but not so for the remainder of the Sunday. In the afternoon the focus was on Sunday School for the children, a congregation of 60 children being quite commonplace. They were brought by their parents and left there for the afternoon. As part of the services rehearsals for the 'Cwrdd Plant' (Children's Meeting) or rehearsals for the scripture examinations for the older children were held. Tea was prepared by the women and for many of the children this would be the highlight of Sunday. The children were then collected by their parents when the adults arrived for the evening service.

The end of the evening service did not mean it was time to go home. There would be tea to follow in the vestry followed by members gathering on the pavement outside to discuss news from 'home' or to discuss the movements in the milk trade. This would involve chats about who was selling so many gallons, and who was about to start a business. In other words, this was a community discussing matters that were of common interest; these gatherings were known as 'Jewin Fairs'. They would be followed by a jaunt to Lyons Corner House for a meal or to Hyde Park to join in the open air singing of Welsh hymns.

Denominational fidelity was important. Eluned Jones and her family lived in Tottenham. Although Holloway Chapel was close by, being faithful Independents they went to King's Cross which meant a long No. 59 trolley bus journey.

Gareth Davies has warm memories of Sunday School. He looked forward to the Whitsun trips and the Christmas concerts. He can recall too the meetings of the various county societies like Cardiganshire, Carmarthenshire and Glamorgan held in the London Welsh Centre in Grays Inn Road as well as the eisteddfodau, concerts and dances held there.

Of all the social activities transplanted in London, the eisteddfod proved most popular. By the end of the nineteenth century, the eisteddfod was well established, the vast majority being denominational. Scarcely was there a chapel or church without its eisteddfod or competitive gathering. Without doubt, milk people played a large part in these gatherings. Two National Eisteddfodau were held in London, in 1887 and in 1901. The eisteddfod remained as an essential feature of the life of the London Welsh for most of the twentieth century. In 1932, Jewin Chapel organised an eisteddfod in Shoreditch Town Hall. A comprehensive programme was drawn up including not only the traditional competitions but also, unusually, translations from Welsh to French.

The religious centres not only organised a moral and ethical programme for the new way of life, but they were – and some still survive – social and intellectual centres for the Welsh community. Tabernacle, Kings Cross always maintained a strong cultural connection including speeches by MPs such as Lloyd George and others of similar status. Drama companies competed for years in the National Eisteddfod. All chapels boasted a drama group. The Boro Drama Group, under the leadership of Byron Jones, won the first prize in its section at the Llangefni National Eisteddfod in the thirties. There were all sorts of social events held at the Welsh Centre in Grays Inn Road including dances, Nativity plays, eisteddfodau, mixed and male voice choirs and later table tennis competitions. This Welsh Centre was established in 1930 largely as a meeting place for the exiled Welsh, whatever their profession. By this time, of course, the Welsh milk trade was well established. The Centre, along with the places of worship became a focal point for the social life of the milk community and all the other Welsh exiles. One cannot over-emphasise the influence and enthusiasm that this establishment exercised. In the words of one typical habitué, they created friendships that have lasted until today. According to some, this was the most successful marriage bureau ever.

The cultural societies that flourished before World War II still exist following the same practices among the churches and chapels in today's Wales. Falmouth Road Chapel had a programme in 1951 (the leaflet costing a shilling) opening with a Noson Lawen (Convivial Evening) followed by a full programme of events including plays, eisteddfodau etc. Other chapels held similar activities some of which have survived until today. Harrow Chapel's programme for 2012-13 includes a talk by the NSPCC and The Sailors Mission. Naturally, there were St David's Day activities including visits by male voice choirs from Wales. In 1983, Jewin hosted 'Gwasanaeth y Cysegr' (similar to Songs of Praise) that was recorded for television, as did Boro Chapel in 2013.

Exiles from Wales, when they returned, would be loath to dispense with the social life that was such an integral part of life in the city. Aberystwyth's London Welsh Society continued holding its annual dinner with traditional toasts and musical items until recently. The branch was dissolved in 2013, but the Ceredigion Branch of the London Welsh Society still survives and meets regularly at the London Welsh Centre.

Similarly, Welsh people living in London and holidaying

in Wales wished to meet old friends. Where was the most convenient place to do so? At the local chapel, of course. Ieuan Parry from Blaenplwyf recalls a story of a service at Tabor Chapel, Llangwyryfon, when one of the deacons counted the number of returnees in their dozens.

There were other aspects to social life in London, for instance the connection between Cardiganshire vocalists and the milk trade. Here it suffices to quote from a local newspaper back in the thirties by someone calling himself 'M.E.':

> There is a long established connection between the Cardi vocalists and the dairy trade in London. Many of them spent their time selling milk along the London streets. The latest is Edgar Evans from Cwrtnewydd presently singing the lead with the Covent Garden Opera Company. Before that there was Roscoe Lloyd, Llanwenog and David Evans of Ponterwyd. David now lives in the Deva on Aberystwyth Promenade. His voice remains true despite his 80 years. To hear him singing 'Dafydd y Garreg Wen' is truly a musical experience. He told me the story of an amusing incident at the start of his career when he was performing in one of the London theatres. Suddenly, from the darkness, there came a young voice: 'Cor! Bill! There's our milkie!' Some youngster had recognised David Evans as their milkman.

Apart from the hearth, the chapel was the stronghold of Welsh. As the number of places of worship decreased due to declining membership, the empty buildings were given new functions. Over the years a number of these buildings amalgamated or closed. Today there remain six Presbyterian chapels, two Independent, one Baptist, one

Anglican Church and not one Wesleyan. Charing Cross Chapel was a nightclub in the eighties before becoming the 'Walkabout' Australian pub but is now an art centre. The Tabernacle in King's Cross was sold to the Ethiopian Christian Fellowship. Willesden Green Chapel became The Temple of the True Buddha. Falmouth Road chapel is the home of the Nigerian Church. As was the case in the past with the Welsh, these places have been taken over by immigrants eager to establish community centres where they could worship according to their own customs and language.

The decline among the Welsh chapels in London can be compared with the reason for their early existence as noted at the beginning of this chapter, that is, they served as pieces of a framework used to provide a moral standard for young people, a focus for worship in a new and strange environment. Today's immigrant is a more sophisticated and self-confident person than his predecessors and as such doesn't feel the need for a kindred social habitat. This, together with the general decline in public worship could be responsible for the present situation in London. However, the Rev Llewelyn Williams, in his book on the history of Tabernacl Chapel, King's Cross, maintains:

> It is said that the vocation of the latest immigrants are different from that of those that filled our Welsh chapels from 1870-1920. Came the day of the combines, and the numbers of the individual dairyman declined – they formed the backbone of our Welsh chapels in London.

Ironically, as the number of milkmen declined, a Welsh day school was opened in London in 1957; this was too late for generations of dairymen's children. But a different influx of

Welsh began to arrive after the war, teachers that came straight from college. As Professor Emrys Jones said:

> Wales exported teachers in vast numbers and London County Council was a generous employer. There was hardly a school without a Taff on the staff.

But that is another story.

Milk and Water

In Dylan Thomas' 'Under Milk Wood', published in 1954, we find Captain Cat musing as he listens to the voices and sounds of the little town of Llaregub. Says the old Captain:

> Ocky Milkman on his round. I will say this, his milk is fresh as the dew. Half dew it is

The assertion that milk sold in the London streets was diluted with water is deeply rooted in Welsh folklore. Often has it been said and heard:

> The only thing I know about the Welsh in London is that they made a lot of money by selling water in milk.

or:

> No-one would have been any the wiser had they added water.

In Ponthrydfendigaid, the village where he was brought up, Sir David James is still referred to by some as the man who made a fortune by selling water in London. Possibly these references were no more than music hall jokes or quips on a 'Noson Lawen' stage in Wales. But they have no substance, at least not during the twentieth century.

Charles Dickens wrote a short story in 1850 with the title 'The Cow with the Iron Tail'. The iron tail referred to a pump in a yard in High Holborn and perhaps there is some substance to the allegation back in the nineteenth century when watering milk was practised. The custom became the subject of leg-pulling, and it remains so. Among the jests, for example, it is alleged that it was a Welshman from Clwyd, Sir

An early milk dispensing machine
(Dilys Scott)

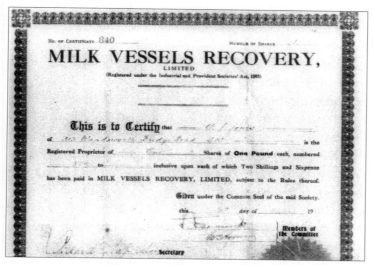

A share certificate of a milk bottle collecting company,
belonging to O. J. Jones, 313 Wandsworth Road
(Emrys Jones)

Hugh Myddleton who brought clean water to London and that it was another Welshman – from Cardiganshire – in the nineteenth and twentieth century-who added a little milk to it, and thus adding as to the myth of describing the pump in the yard as 'the cow with the iron tail'. It is also rumoured that dairymen in the nineteenth century would add a little warm water in order to show that their milk was fresh.

The variations in the quality of milk during the early years were accepted facts. The custom of street vending inevitably meant variations in the quality of milk because of the methods of delivery. In his study of *The London Welsh Milk Trade in 1860-1900*, E. H. Wentham states that there were dangers in street selling arising from ladling the milk from a wide-necked churn. Early customers then got the cream while the later customers received little more than skimmed milk. The situation possibly improved with the advent of locked churns with taps at the bottom. However, that only turned the problem upside down with the early customers getting the skimmed milk and the later customers the cream. The sellers themselves were plagued by dishonest providers who sold more milk than was allocated to them by adding water.

Watering milk was made an offence in law under the Adulteration of Food and Drink Act of 1860. Very few of the local authorities invoked the powers granted to them until they were compelled to do so by the Adulteration of Food, Drink and Drugs Act of 1872. However, suspicion of dilution was much easier than proving it as the composition was so variable.

Preventing dilution was but one step forward in ensuring milk of a better quality. Cowsheds, centres for handling milk and dairy equipment became open to inspection with the advent of the Public Health and the Sale of Food and Drugs Act of 1875, and when regulations

A council public analyst employee collects a shop sample of milk for analysis
(Gwenllian Jenkins)

relating to the Infectious Diseases (Animals) Act of 1878 were published, standards were set in basic hygiene were imposed.

The situation changed drastically in the twentieth century. Public health standards were strict and were just as strictly implemented. A bottle of milk could be taken for examination without any warning. The milk would be divided between three bottles, one for the dairyman and two for analysis. Any sign of dilution or skimming could lead to local newspaper reporting, loss of customers, goodwill and as a result, livelihood.

Despite this, and the legal situation described above, and because of the long history of dilution allied with the complexity of the law, folk lore involving dilution became a mindset among the general population. That, doubtless, was what led one dairyman to include on his invoices until late in the last century the words:

Daily family deliveries of Fresh, Pure Milk. Analysis welcomed.

Why, in the case of a programme on the milk trade in London in the second half of the twentieth century was it considered necessary to congratulate the author for not once mentioning the possibility of milk being diluted or watered down? For me, connecting such activities with the Welsh in London is an insult, just as it would be so to connect people with avoidance of the payment of income tax.

The myth was perpetuated in an unfortunate way in the *Aberystwyth Observer* on 9 July 1904. What was headlined as a slighting observation was made by a Mr Fordham, a J.P. in London who alleged that 90 per cent of those summonsed for diluting milk were Welsh. He wished to be informed whether it was only the Welsh that were diluting milk or was it the Welsh people who had a monopoly of all milk sales? The prosecuting solicitor said that Welsh people certainly favoured the milk trade. It is sad that the report did not carry a stronger objection or any relevant statistical analysis. On the other hand, might it be a residue of what had been accepted practice in the previous century but before the stricter regulations had been imposed and accepted. It at least confirms the strong presence of the Welsh in the London milk trade.

It is obvious that folk memory is long and that the problems of milk vending in the nineteenth century has lingered long in people's minds. It is very possible to compare diluting milk in the twentieth century with speeding drivers in our time. Speeding beyond the law, a law not always obeyed, with the acceptance of the possibility of having to face the consequences.

The law has always been interested in implementing

rules concerning sales. At the beginning of the twentieth century shops were not permitted to sell whilst officially closed, as on a Wednesday afternoon. An interesting court case occurred as a result of implementing the Shopping Act of 1912 when the legitimacy of a milk vending machine outside a London Welshman's shop in Willesden was challenged. There was disagreement amongst the Middlesex magistrates who rejected the charge. But the matter was taken further in an effort to establish whether operating such a machine, even though it was outside a closed shop, was legal. The appeal was rejected on the basis that a similar machine in a nearby railway station had set a precedent. As a result, at least one 'iron cow' became legal.

Another bone of contention, although it did not involve the law, was that concerning lost milk bottles. All sellers had

E.W.Morgan & Sons
Somerset Farm Dairies
25,Tamworth Street, Fulham, SW6
(With the Weights & Measures Man)

A council public analyst employee collects a street barrow sample of milk
(Glyn Lewis collection)

their name inscribed on their bottles. But 'stray' bottles belonging to one vendor were frequently found among the bottles belonging to another vendor. It was possible to insure against this by buying shares in Milk Vessels Recovery Ltd. who undertook to return such misplaced bottles to their rightful owners. In 1929, Mr O.J. Jones of 313 Wandsworth Bridge Road was registered as the Registered Owner of one share in the company that was worth one pound.

Gwyn Pickering, who still lives in London, recalls the story of a friend who was repeatedly being warned by the police for washing his milk cart in the street. This was contrary to one of the Westminster Council's by-laws. Because he chose to ignore the warnings so often, he was summoned to appear before Marylebone Magistrates. When asked why he insisted on washing the cart in the street rather than in the yard his reply was:

> It would be easier for me to put the yard in the cart than to put the cart in the yard.

The case was dismissed. What a shame that today's stage comedians can't be as humorous as that milkman from Soho!

The Shadow of the War

As the bombs of World War II began to reign on London, hundreds of children were evacuated to the safety of rural areas, many to Wales. A number of these, especially children of dairymen, had the advantage of already being used to visiting relatives whilst on holiday. But when war was declared they were sent to the safety of their relatives for the duration of the conflict. Among them was Johnny Lewis who was sent to Dihewyd. Glanville and Emlyn Davies, the children of Jack Davies, from Glynarthen and the two sons of Jack Davies and his wife Sally were sent to Neath. Marjorie Hughes was sent to Llanfihangel-y-creuddyn and Betty Evans to Felinfach. London Welsh families sent their children to relatives in Wales. But one example can be given of the generosity of one Welsh family to accept children entrusted to them by parents aware only of the trust and sincerity of members of that family. Rachel Jane Jones, from Sarnau, had gone to London directly on leaving school in 1928 to work with a dairy family but decided to return to Wales on the outbreak of war. She took with her four children of her customers, all of school age, and at the last minute had a baby thrust into her arms with the injunction, 'Take my baby to safety!'. That group of five were cared for by the Sarnau family for the duration of the war, returning to London with little English but fluent Welsh. These are but a few examples of children who spent long periods away from their parents, but who were kept safe.

The severe raids on London started on 7 September 1940 and years of bombing would follow. Jewin Chapel was one of the buildings to suffer on 18th September 1940. The bombings eased when the German bombers were diverted to the Eastern Front. The worst was over, at least until the devastating raids of the V1 and V2 rockets at the end of the war.

D. R. and E. Daniels in their Westminster shop
(Margaret Thomas)

Trefor and Mair Morgan in their Portobello Shop
(Trefor and Mair Morgan)

Dewi Morgan from Bethania, previously referred to, was one who spent the war years in London. He failed his medical examination twice and was rejected for military service. However, with the market at its lowest, he ventured to buy J.J. Jones and Sons' business in Wick Road in February 1944. In an article in the *Cambrian News* on 24 April 1987 he wrote:

> It was very difficult at the beginning. Because of the evacuation and the destruction of homes we were down to sales of ten gallons a day. Then the Council decided to build hundreds of prefabs after the war and when we sold the business in 1953 we were selling 1,000 gallons a day.

The war affected every aspect of life and work in London. Pre-war the dairyman's aim was to serve and answer the need of as many homes as possible. By this means the goodwill and thus the value of the business was increased. If it were possible to reach a customer's home by bike, that meant another name on the book, and in so doing earning extra money. The result of this during the pre-war period was that an area could be served by a number of dairymen, and a particular street could be getting delivery from a number of dairies. This was the uneconomic consequence of the desire to build a business.

Ironically, the impact of the war provided the solution. The answer was to create zones or blocks. Rearrangement of delivery catchments was organised resulting in confining an individual business to a specific area. However, this redistribution was done ensuring that the total quantity of milk supplied and so the value of the dairy was safeguarded. This reorganisation was welcomed as reasonable. Even so, the Co-op was exempted from the arrangement. The bonus or 'divi' was too much an attraction. The reorganisation reduced the number of milk rounds thus releasing men to join the armed services.

Rationing food meant that one had to register with a specific shop and exchange coupons for different goods. It was only in that shop that food could be purchased by a registered customer because the Food Office would not authorise more than was sufficient for registered customers, but with a little bit extra for servicemen home on leave.

The aim of continuity of service still held good. If the wholesaler could supply milk to the dairymen, then the dairymen were determined to pass the product on to the customer, come what might. Whatever the impact of the war, the dairymen regarded it as their duty to ensure that full bottles would be left on the doorsteps.

Dan Thomas and his wife Getta from Cwmtydu kept a dairy in Tottenham Street. They spent every bombing night sheltering in Goodge Street underground station; they used the bags that held the day's sale receipts as pillows for their heads. Every morning they returned to the shop to resume business as usual. When war was declared Mrs Eileen Brigshaw of Aberarth's father volunteered with the Royal Navy Police in the Admiralty. By working at night he was able to return home every morning to carry out the milk round. So strict were the rules that Dilys Scott's father had to appear before a series of tribunals to justify staying at home to provide milk for his customers despite the fact that he served nightly as an Air Raid Warden.

There are countless examples of relatives from Wales – mostly women – leaving home for London to help with businesses because milkmen had been called up by the services, for example, Eilir Daniel of Llandeilo's great aunt went to London to help a relative temporarily but stayed throughout the war. Gwynn Evans' family kept a dairy in

Bessie Jones and colleague take the milk round in WW2.
Milk bottling took place in the sandbagged basement on the right.
(Henry Jones)

Holland Park. His father was called up, so his mother went to London to help.

The air raids had a devastating effect on businesses and livelihoods. The Davies family from Glynarthen, who had already sent their two sons to the safety of Neath, faced the crisis by travelling nightly to Slough and returning to their dairy every morning to deliver milk. This was a practice that lasted for many months. Then, towards the end of 1944, whilst everyone was abed, a bomb landed in the middle of the street opposite destroying one end of the shop completely. Their lives were saved by the fact that the beams were supported by the two opposite walls rather than by the gable end walls. However, the building was condemned as being unsafe and was ordered to be demolished completely. In seconds, the family had lost everything without any hope of compensation. They left to join their children in Neath and started a new business in haulage.

Iwan Jones of Lampeter's father saw his business slump from 600 to 100 customers because of the bombing and the evacuation. He had no option but to return to Wales leaving it all behind.

Margaret Davies, a member of the Darren Fawr family, kept a business in Boswell Road. Margaret ran her own business while her husband was in the army but she was joined by family members. They sheltered from the bombing in Holborn underground station. One morning they returned to find that the shop had been bombed. Margaret was close to giving birth and there was no choice but to return to Wales for the birth.

One Sunday evening, Oriel Jones from Llanfihangel-ar-arth' s family was attending the service at King's Cross Chapel. They returned home to find their home and business completely destroyed by an air raid. Both the building and the business had been reduced to rubble.

Marjorie Hughes from Llandre in her memoirs of Llandre Chapel, Bow Street describes the effects of the war on her parent's business. Although only eight years old at the time she still remembers the Anderson Shelters and the atmosphere of the blackout. She was sent away to safety to Llanfihangel-y-Creuddyn but a bomb caused considerable damage to the family shop. The ceiling collapsed and the windows were blown out. Yet, despite the damage and the loss of the electric supply for a long time, the shop had to be kept open.

Betty Evans of Aberporth's parents kept eight milking cows at their business in the East End. One night their home was bombed. Everything was destroyed. All the cows were killed and the only choice was to return home to Felinfach. Such events were commonplace; there was no compensation of any kind and it meant having to start all over again.

There are many interesting tales of how many families strove to try and live a normal life while having to avoid the bombing. Ann Edwards can recall customers joining her family in the shop. An escape route had been fashioned by breaking through the wall into next door's tobacco shop; covering the opening was a large oil painting. When the siren was heard, those in the two buildings would congregate and there, and while awaiting the 'all clear' sing and dance, doing their utmost to ignore what was happening outside and above them.

To Peggy Beaven, the daughter of John and Margaret Jacob who kept a dairy in Willesden, the war proved to be a blessing in disguise. She felt that the block system saved her parents' business. It put an end to having to travel miles in order to deliver a pint or two. She also felt that the rationing regime had been of benefit as it meant that every customer had to register with a particular shop. There were other improvements also. The milk was delivered already bottled. Her parents also managed to buy a fridge and to exchange the old milk pram for a light electric milk float.

The end of the war saw the whole social pattern and marketing processes change completely. Damage to buildings was on a massive scale and some businesses had disappeared completely overnight. The creation of zones introduced as part of the milk regulating programme had changed the whole pattern of life for the dairymen.

Bowen Williams' family from New Barnet had experience of the milk trade through both World Wars. Bowen's father, John Morgan Williams left Llanrhystud when he was 17 years old to work for a wholesaler at the end of the nineteenth century. His mother, the eldest of five children from Bronnant had left for London to work as a maid. They married at the beginning of the last century and started a business in Stockwell. They worked throughout the First World War experiencing the terror of the Zeppelins. From 1912 to 1921, milk was imported form Somerset in 17 gallon churns and sold directly to the customers who brought their own jugs.

Bowen was born in 1920. The family moved back to Wales but after 12 years they had to return to London because of the depression. They took over Park Dairies in Hornsey, a business involving three milk rounds.

During World War II the mother had to run the business with the oldest son, who also worked in the ambulance service following his time in the army. Bowen himself enlisted in the RAF but at the completion of his time there he returned to the family business. He is in a perfect position to compare conditions before and after World War II. The zone plan and the hardship of war resulted in confining the number of milk rounds to two and because of wartime regulations they had to give up the early pre-seven round. But matters improved and after the war the number of rounds increased and the early morning round was restored. By now, milk arrived in bottles and the old hand-pushed carts gave way to electric trolleys. Eventually the business was sold in 1985 to the Lord Rayleigh Farm Company bringing to an end 53 years of dairying.

The majority of dairies had existed from sometime way before the war. Of the dairymen who had to leave owing to the war, only a few returned to the trade and very few started a new life in the city.

Trefor and Mair Morgan from Bwlchllan were exceptions. Having begun farming in Cwmann under difficult circumstances they decided to join the London milk trade and purchased a business in Portobello in 1962. The business consisted of a traditional dairy and shop and was bought through the services of a Welsh agent, David Jones, There were two daily rounds. Their early rounds-man was Idris Davies from Llannon and Trefor himself took the second. Mair ran the shop by herself from 7.00 am to 7.00 pm daily. The milk arrived in bottles from large independent dairies – these were plain bottles without the company logo therefore there was no danger of their going astray. Trefor and Mair stayed in business for seven years.

An indication of the great changes that were to come was experienced by the family of Andrew Jones from Llandysul. They went to London in 1959 following a brother who had left ten years earlier. But rather than being content with merely delivering milk to doorsteps, this family decided to branch out. They succeeded in securing the contract to supply milk to the Olympic Stadium in the way later dairymen such as Lewis, Jones and Morgan today supply hotels and businesses.

The war was a turning point in milk marketing. More and more dairymen and their families were forced to sell their businesses to the large conglomerates. Many of these families resorted to the bed and breakfast trade. These were often located near the main train stations such as Euston, Victoria and Paddington.

One by one the milk rounds were bought by large companies leaving the smaller shops without income from those sources. This was not enough to be viable. Some owners resorted to selling snacks such as sandwiches to workers in nearby offices. Johnny Lewis from Aberaeron provides a good example. His grandfather, a lead miner from Cwmsymlog, opened a dairy in Blackfriars. The business was inherited by Johnny's father and later by Johnny himself in the fifties. He had to sell the milk-round to another Lewis from Llwyncelyn and concentrate on selling sandwiches to passing trade and to bulk catering though he still sold milk

D. R. and E. Daniels black-outed Westminster shop
(Margaret Thomas)

over the counter. He also turned to professional boxing as a welter or light heavyweight. Eventually the dairy was sold to an Italian and ended up as a café.

One of the last traditional businesses was that of D. R. and B. Daniels in Westminster. They started a dairy business in Morton Terrace in 1931 and stayed until 1995 before retiring to Wales like many other dairy folk. In an article in the 'Western Mail' they wrote of their last days in London. They described their working conditions – starting at 5.00 am by bottling the milk and then working in the shop all day. Eventually, they gave up the milk round and only sold milk over the counter. They also sold bread, cereals and general groceries. Mr Daniel proudly described how he once prevented a burglary.

The bombing and the consequent rebuilding had a devastating effect on the dairies with the result that very few now remain to remind us of their existence. However, one can name three businesses that managed to survive the upheaval of war.

The Lewis family business was established in 1928 by Lewis Lewis from Pennant and his wife Gwladys. Their son and daughter in law, Glyn and Iris, continued running the business as a traditional dairy until they sold the milk rounds. The retained the shop and began delivering milk to restaurants and hotels. The shop closed seven years ago and nowadays concentrates on delivering milk to city centre restaurants with a fleet of vans operating out of Emma Street, Bethnal Green, where the main office is situated. It is run by John and Edward Lewis, grandchildren of the founders.

The Morgans' milk company was established by Morris Evan Morgan in 1894 and – as in the case of the Lewis Brothers – it continues as an independent milk company. In 1947 it was bought from a member of the family by Mair and Ieuan Morgan and is nowadays owned by their sons, Gareth and Geraint. They still deliver milk to the door in the area around their centre of operation in Fulham but their business is mainly wholesale to clients that include restaurants, caterers and offices as well. They now also supply on-line deliveries.

The third business to survive is that of the Jones Brothers in The City of London Dairy. The business was established in Jewry Street by Henry Jones and his family who left Borth near Aberystwyth in 1877. Henry married Sarah Anne Morgan from Clarach. They then moved to a business in Stoney Lane. Following their demise – we have already referred to Sarah's return to be buried in Llanfihangel Genau'r Glyn – the business was inherited by two sons. During the war the sisters took over the business while their brothers served in the armed forces. After the war, the Stoney Lane dairy was demolished and new premises opened in Middlesex Street with a shop selling dairy products. Delivery to private houses has ceased and the business is now wholesale only. It is in the hands of the fourth generation of three partners, Trefor, Catherine and Henry Jones with a fifth generation awaiting its turn.

Meanwhile, a few dairy premises remain. Though their function has changed, conservation policy has ensured that at least one is preserved. In Amwell Street one finds Lloyd and Son's Dairy. A photograph of the shop interior is typical of what would have been seen in the thirties. One feature common to many such shops, and can be seen here, is a pair of a Castlemartin cow's horns, an echo of the drovers. And in Camden, T. Evans' old dairy at 35 Warren Street on the corner of Conway Street remains with its original tiling and rails still in place. The last Welsh owner of the shop was Mrs Evans, who retired in 2000. Nowadays a Turkish family runs a business there. The building dates from around 1793. Plaques in the shop remind one of the days when it was opened as a dairy around 1916. What is today the entrance to the Mews leads to where the cattle and their keepers would have been housed. Today the whole is a Listed Grade II building. To adapt Dafydd Iwan's words:

RY'N NI YNA O HYD!
WE ARE STILL THERE!

The End

A timeline can be drawn when recording the history of the milk trade in London. It follows the economic and social history of a small area of Wales.

The drovers provided London with cattle bred on Welsh pastures while the cattle keepers provided milk for the increasing population of the city. The trade was ultimately adopted and developed by and large by a population of dairymen, mostly from Cardiganshire, but with some from other parts of Wales. Later economic pressures led to their demise and they were succeeded by ventures that survive to this day in the hands of people who are proud of their roots and origin.

One or two comments can be offered. When two or three members of old Cardi families get together, the conversation often turns to a network of family connections, all of them with the experience of having been involved with the Welsh milk trade in London. Inevitably, the conversation will turn to asking what chapel or church was frequented. Part of this relationship was the decision and determination to raise their children in a Welsh atmosphere in London with the Sunday School being an influential centre of major importance. In some instances the desire to return to Wales proved so strong that families returned home when the children were very small. Among these were Trefor and Mair Morgan from Aberystwyth.

Trefor and Mair, as previously mentioned, were among the few who ventured into the milk trade after World War II. They saw for themselves the impact of the coming of the hypermarket and the vast changes in the nature of the business. The large conglomerations swallowed up the small establishments with those who had previously selling milk and shop goods turned to opening bed and breakfast premises or returning to the old country. Trefor and Mair returned.

They farmed in Wales and sold milk in London within the same decade and so comparison of occupations and conditions are valid. When I asked Trefor which of the two occupations, in his opinion, was the hardest he answered without any hesitation:

> Selling milk – there was no respite at weekends neither was there between seasons.

But 'home' always meant Wales – a place to retire to and a place that would receive contributions to good causes.

The milkmen have disappeared one by one. The London Welsh population is now largely professional. Life has followed the general trend and the influence of the places of worship has declined.

The generation that followed the dairymen has not been as limited in its choice of occupation. Among them we find representatives of the professions – doctors, solicitors, engineers and teachers. They have succeeded by adapting their inheritance of the strength and intelligence derived from their ancestors to secure entrance into a broader society whilst maintaining a fitting pride their lineage in the milk trade.

This is a group of photos taken by my mother – as were the two of Norah and Bet on page 71. She always had a camera handy to take work-related scenes and her work, along with some of rural 30s agriculture, is in Casgliad y Werin (The People's Collection) in the National Library of Wales.

Dilys, Idwal and Ceri, staff in the Clapham business

Stan Gannaway, one of the roundsmen with a crate of bottles to wash

Outside the Clapham shop

An outing on a shop closing afternoon to Runnymead: my father, two of our live-in maids – and me

Appendix 1

Hen Borthmyn

Ap Lewis
(David Evan Davies)

1

Mae Cymru a'i helynt yn annwyl i mi
Ei chymoedd feithrinodd enwogion o fri,
Ymhlith y rhai hynny sy heddiw tan gŵys
Myn hanes gofnodi hen borthmyn Llancrwys.

Da dewrion a dwys,
Da Dewrion a dwys,
Difyrrus eu hanes
Oedd porthmyn Llancrwys.

2

Mae Ffair Ffaldybrenin yn ango ers tro,
A darfod yn gyflym mae ffeiriau y fro,
Does sôn am Ffordd Lloegr yn awr, na'r 'trw-hê' –
Y trên â'u diddymodd, daeth Sais yn eu lle.

3

Am fechgyn Llangurig does nemor ddim sôn,
Bron darfod bob copa mae porthmyn sir Fôn,
Fe gollodd Tregaron ei jocys yn llwyr,
Pa beth yw y rheswm, oes undyn a ŵyr?

4

Wrth neud eu cyflogau roedd gweision y plwy
Yn hawlio, i Loegr, ryw siwrne neu ddwy;
Y crydd gyda'r teiliwr a'r gwehydd fai'n cal
Siwrneion bob hydre i chwyddo eu tâl.

Old Drovers

Ap Lewis
(David Evan Davies)

1

Wales and her tales are so close to my heart,
Her valleys have nourished great men of renown,
Among those who today lie under the clay
We must name the drovers of old Llanycrwys.

Fat cattle and stout,
Fat cattle and stout,
Much fabled their story,
Those men of Llancrwys.

2

Ffaldybrenin's old fair is forgotten of late,
And soon many others will share the same fate
Like the old London Road and shouts of 'troo-hey!'
The train came along bringing English this way.

3

The lads of Llangurig aren't mentioned today,
The Anglesey drovers have gone the same way,
Tregaron has lost all it's jockeys as well.
Whatever the reason, there's no-one can tell.

4

To make up their wages, the servants of old
Would venture to journey to London, we're told;
The cobbler, the tailor and weaver, they say,
Would go every autumn to bolster their pay.

5

Cyfnewid mae ffasiwn yn gyflym o hyd,
Cyfnewid, ran hynny mae pobol y byd;
Y rhaff rawn a'r bicas sy'n awr heb un iws,
A'r fforch at bedoli, yr hoelion a'r ciws.

6

Cychwynnai y porthmyn yn writgoch ac iach
I ddilyn y ffeiriau, tua dechre Mis Bach;
Ac yna trwy'r flwyddyn, ar hyd ac ar led,
Yn prynu a gwerthu tra mynd ar y trêd.

7

O ffeiriau sir Benfro, da mawrion i gyd,
A'u cyrnau gan fwyaf yn llathed o hyd;
O Hwlffordd, Treletert, a Narberth, rhai braf,
O Grymych, Maenclochog a Thŷ-Gwyn-ar-Daf.

8

O Lanarth, o Lanbed, Ffair Rhos a Thalsarn,
O Ledrod, Llandalis, y delent yn garn,
O ffeiriau Llanbydder, Penuwch a Chross Inn,
Da duon, da gleision, ac ambell un gwyn.

9

O ffeiriau Caerfyrddin, da perton ac ir,
Ac ambell f'ewynnog o waelod y sir;
Doi da Castell Newydd a Chynwil i'r lan
At dda Dyffryn Tywi i gyd i'r un man.

10

Nôl cael at ei gilydd y nifer yn llawn,
A'r gofiaid bedoli pob ewin yn iawn,
Cychwynnai y fintai yn hwylus eu bron
Y 'guide' yn bryderus, a'r haliers yn llon.

5

The fashions are changing so quickly, but then,
The same can be said of the ways of all men,
The hemp rope and pickaxe today have no use
Like the old shoeing prong, the nails and the cues.

6

The drovers would set off with healthy red cheeks
To follow the fairs around February's first weeks,
And thence all year-long, they roamed here and there
With their buying and selling while the trading was fair.

7

From the Pembrokeshire fairs, cows all fat and gross,
Their horns mostly measured a full yard across,
From Narberth, Treletert and Haverfordwest,
From Crymych, Maenclochog and Whitland, the best.

8

From Llanarth and Lampeter, Talsarn and Ffair Rhos,
From Lledrod, Llanddalis, in rows upon rows,
Llanybydder, Penuwch and Cross Inn, what a sight
Some blacks and some blues, and one or two whites.

9

From the fairs of Carmarthen, fine cows in a flow,
And one or two barrens from further below,
From Newcastle Emlyn and Cynwil, in throng,
To the Vale of the Tywi, they all came along.

10

With the cows herded up, their number complete,
Blacksmiths would shoe every hoof quick and neat,
Then the drove with new vigour would lithely depart,
The guide with foreboding, the hauliers with heart.

11

Roedd nifer o haliers dan ofal y 'guide',
A hwn oedd yn trefnu y cyfan, gan wneud
Yr oll o'r taliadau am gaeau a tholl
A chyfrif amdanynt yn gyflawn heb goll.

12

Yr haliers rai troeon yn borthmyn yr aent
Os benthyg peth arian yn rhywle a gaent;
A llawer hen geffyl rôl ffaelu'n ei waith
Ddoi'n ebol lled hoyw cyn terfyn y daith.

13

Drwy dref Llanymddyfri, dros Lwydlo a'r Wy,
Ymadael â Chymru i ddychwelyd byth mwy,
Mae ffyrdd yn ymledu a'r borfa'n brashau,
Yr haliers yn llaesu, a'r da yn tewhau.

14

Un tro pan oedd Rhysyn yn halier i'w dad,
Fe syrthiodd yn sydyn dros ymyl y bad
I ganol yr afon, ond glaniodd yn iach
Wrth gynffon yr eidon yng nghafan Twm Bach.

15

Cychwynnai y porthmyn cyn toriad y wawr
I'r ffeiriau yn Lloger ar ben y 'Coach Mawr',
Drwy Henffordd a Ledbury thiroedd y gwair
I Gent neu Northampton, 'nôl fel byddai'r ffair.

16

Os digon o mofyn, fe werthid yn rhwydd
Dda mawrion yn gynta, ac yna rhai blwydd,
Rôl talu amdanynt a'u danfon yn iawn,
Roedd pob un yn llawen a'i logell yn llawn.

11

The guide, as a rule, was in charge of the crew,
And he, as the foreman, would pay what was due
For pasture and toll fees all along the way,
And this he would do without any delay.

12

The hauliers themselves could be drovers one day
Should they manage to borrow on top of their pay;
And many an old nag, its usefulness gone,
Would feel like a colt er'e the journey was done.

13

Through the town of Llandovery, Ludlow and Wye,
Bidding Wales a last, sad good-bye,
The roads now are wider, there's pasture about,
The hauliers relax and the cattle grow stout.

14

Long ago, when young Rhys was a haulier of note,
While crossing the river, he fell from the boat
As it cossed in mid-stream, but he landed just aft
Holding on to a calf's tail from Twm Bach's old craft.

15

The drovers set off just as morning approached
To the fairs on the roof of the famous Big Coach
Through Hereford, Ledbury and 'lands of the hay'
To Kent or Northampton, when came the fair day.

16

If business was good, the bidding would flow,
Firstly the fat cows, then the yearlings would go,
And after the payment and the cows sent away,
Full pockets and joy marked the end of the day.

17
I blith yr aneirod ym merw y ffair
Aeth ambell i fustach – un dwyflwydd neu dair –
A dwedid fod weithiau gyfnewid yn bod -
Roedd llawer yn methu adnabod y nod.

18
Am y cynta'i fynd adre yn awr fyddai'r gamp
Yn hwyr ac yn fore ar ddwytroed – yn dramp.
Ceid te a pheth licer, ond peidiwch â sôn,
Cyfrwyau a ffrwyni, neu ddillad o'r pôn.

19
Tra'n croesi yr afon i'r gwëydd rhoddwyd sen
Am ddychwel i Gymru a dimau dros ben.
'I bob gwlad ei harian,' medd William, bid siŵr,
Gan daflu y ddimau yn ôl dros y dŵr.

20
Wrth ddod at Dŷ Hetti yn fore rhyw ddydd,
Fe'i clywsent hi'n gwaeddi yn rhuddgoch a rhydd:
'Does gen i ddim diod, darfyddodd yn llwyr,
A phryd câ'i beth eto, y mowredd a ŵyr.'

21
'O, wel,' ebe William, 'yr oedd hi'n go wan
Pan o'n i'n mynd heibio y ffordd hyn i'r lan,
Mi wedes wrth Dafydd, mab Teimoth y go
Ma darfod y neithe'i os na cheise'i dro.'

22
Ar ddiwedd y ffeiriau pan ddaethent ynghyd
I wneud y cyfrifon dan gronglwyd fawr glyd,
Ceid adrodd helyntion am oriau'n ddi-ball –
Pob un ar ei orau i drechu y llall.

17

In amongst all the heiffers in the heat of the flow
Would wander a steer- a yearling or so-
And sometimes, it's said, a switch would be planned-
There were many who couldn't decipher the brand.

18

It then was a race to reach home at full pace
Morning or night on two legs – what a race!
There was tea and strong ale – but better refrain
From mentioning saddles abandoned – such pain!

19

While crossing the river, mocked was the weaver
For coming back home with a halfpence left over,
'To each land its money,' said Will, what a giver!
While tossing his halfpence back over the river.

20

One day, as they reached Hetty's Cottage in force,
She shouted out loudly all redfaced and hoarse:
'I've run out of beer, every drop has gone flat
When I can have more, only Heaven knows that.'

21

'Ah, well!' muttered William, 'she was pretty low
When I last passed this way just a few days ago,
I mentioned to Dafydd, son of Teimoth the shop
That dead she would be without having a drop.'

22

At the end of a fair, when they all came together
To note their accounts safe and dry from the weather,
All the tales of the journey they'd try to recount,
Each trying to better the other's account.

23

Ar derfyn yr hanes, dymunol im' yw
Fod coffa amdanynt hyd heddiw yn fyw;
A bod y rhinweddau oedd eiddo hwynt-hwy
Fyw eto ym mywyd trigolion y plwy.

Roedd Tomos Phillips Ochorbryn
Yn wr go dyn am fargen;
A Jones Ro-wen wrth brynu da
Enillodd lawer sofren;
Am ddaoedd mân a phrisoedd is –
Ben Lewis Cwmcelynen.

Rhown enw Davies Troedybryn
I lawr fan hyn fel porthmon,
A William Davies gynt o'r Llwyn
A dau o'i fwynaidd feibion;
Bu Price Werndigaid gyda hwy
Yn tramwy gwlad y Saeson.

Nathaniel Edwards – enwog un,
A'i fechgyn yn eu helfen,
Mistir Morgans o Flaentwrch
A'i 'guide' o Fwlch-y-gilwen;
A Gwr y Siop gylymai'n dyn
Y gadwyn am y goeden.

Roedd Dafydd Harries Blaen-y-clawdd
Yn borthmon hawdd i 'daro',
A John Walters Esgercrwys
Fu'n borthmon dwys yn delo,
A Joseph Jones, un annwyl oedd –
Gan luoedd gaiff ei gofio.

23

At the end of the tale, it's a pleasure to say
That memories of these men remain to this day;
And that the virtues they held in times that were good
Live on in the folk of today's neighbourhood.

Tomos Phillips Ochorbryn
Was quite a man for bargains;
And Jones Ro-wen, while buying cows
Earned himself many sovereigns;
For myriad cows for lower fees,
Ben Lewis Cwmcelynen.

We mention Davies, Troedybryn
Down here as a drover,
And William Davies, once of Llwyn
And both his sons, so gentle;
And Price Werndigaid spent much time
Walking with them through England.

Nathaniel Edwards – famous man
And sons, all full of vigour;
Mister Morgan of Blaentwrch
And his guide from Bwlch-y-gilwen;
And the Shopkeeper tying tight
The chain around the tree-trunk.

Dafydd Harries Blaen-y-clawdd
Was easy in a bargain;
And John Walters Esgercrwys
Was deep in drover dealing;
And Joseph Jones, much loved was he,
Remembered with great feeling.

Caed Lewis Lewis Pantycrug
Yn ddeler diddig ddigon,
Gŵr Brynmawr ddanfonodd lu
O dda i wlad y Saeson;
Roedd Godre Rhos yn brynwr ta'r
A gŵr Brynarau-Gleision.

Bu Daniel Davies o Dynant
Do, droeon bant yn Lloeger,
Daeth Howell Jones a gŵr Ddolwen
Yn berchen arian lawer,
A Tomos Blaen-cwm-pedol fu
Am flwyddi lu yn ddeler.

Pedolwyr gwych am isel bris
Oedd Isaac Rees a'i fechgyn;
Tra Dafi'r go a Jaci'r Ram
Na hidient fawr am undyn;
Ond nid oedd gwell rhai yn y trêd
Na gofiaid Ffaldybrenin.

Ni chlywir mwy am borthmyn clust
Na chwaith am 'list to order',
Na chlinc y ciws ar draed y da
Fai'n mynd bob ha' i Loeger;
Ni welir mwy y ffrwst a'r brys
Am hoelion Rhys y Nailer.

Pa le mae Barnet fawr ei bri
A Naseby a West Haddin,
Neu Harley Bush a Harley Row
Ac Ingaston a Maldin?
Y ffeiriau aeth, eu meth a'u moes,
Darfyddodd oes y porthmyn.

Lewis Lewis Pantycrug
Was a very placid dealer;
The man from Brynmawr sent a host
Of cattle on to England;
And he from Godre Rhos was keen
As was he from Brynaerau-Gleision.

Daniel Davies of Tynant
Quite often went to England;
Howell Jones and he of Dolwen
Both became very wealthy;
And Tomos Blaen-cwm-pedol was
For many years a dealer.

Shoers renowned for a fair price
Were Isaac Rees and sons;
While Davy the Smith and Jack the Ram
Cared not a fig for anyone;
But none was better in the trade
Than the smiths of Ffaldybrenin.

We hear no more of droving by ear
Nor hear of list to order,
No sounds of clinking from the shoes
That walked each summer to England;
No more we see the rush and haste
For nails from Rhys the Nailer.

Where now is Barnet of renown
And Naseby and West Haddin,
Or Harley Bush and Harley Row
And Ingaston and Maldin?
The fairs have gone, their fame and fun,
The drovers' era's vanished.

Appendix 2

Here we have an example of the charges incurred by the drover Dafydd Jenkins in droving cattle from Cardiganshire to London in 1839.

Jonathan Accounts (1839)	£	s.	d.
Cwmdulas House		5	0
Abergwesyn Tavern		15	0
Boy drive the beast		2	0
Newbridge Tavern			6
Llandrindod grass		13	6
Smith, tavern			6
Smith, grass		17	0
Maesyfed gate		1	6
Pay John for shoeing	1	1	0
Kington gate		3	0
Kington grass		18	0
Half-the-road gate		3	0
Llanllern gate		2	6
Westinton grass	1	0	0
Westinton grass		5	9
Westinton gate		3	0
Bromyard gate		3	6
Bontwillt gate		2	3
Bontwillt tavern		17	3
Worcester gate		5	0
Worcester tavern			6
Worcester tavern		2	6
Wilbercastle tavern		18	0
Wilbercastle gate		2	9
Stratford grass		14	6
Stratford tavern		3	0
Stratford gate		2	6

Warwick tavern	18	3
Southam tavern	18	0
Warwick gate	2	6
Windmill tavern	18	0
Windmill gate	2	0
Daventry grass	14	6
Daventry tavern	3	7
Daventry gate	5	0
Northampton tavern	18	0
Northampton gate	2	6
Wellingboro' gate	2	6
Wellingboro' gate	2	6
Wellingboro' tavern	13	6
William Wells tavern	8	6
? gate	2	6

Elstow tavern	1	19	0
Elstow tavern	1	10	6
Man mind beasts		1	6
Egin tavern		16	6
Egin gate		1	6
Hertford tavern		2	6
Hertford gate		2	6
Stansted tavern		13	3
Ongar grass	1	2	0
Ongar tavern		5	0
Chelmsford	1	0	0
Other expenses at fair and return home	2	0	4
	£26	9	5

Appendix 3

Cyngor i'r Porthmyn, gan y Ficer Prichard (1549-1644)

Os d'wyt borthmon dela'n onest,
Tâl yn gywir am a gefaist;
Cadw d'air, na thor addewid;
Gwell nag aur mewn côd yw credid.

Na chais ddala'r tlawd wrth angen,
Na thrachwanta ormod fargen:
Na fargeinia â charn lladron,
Ni ddaw rhad o ddim a feddon.

Gochel brynu mawr yn echwyn,
Pawb ar air a werth yn 'sgymun;
Prynu'n echwyn a wna i borthmon
Ado'r wlad a mynd i'r Werddon.

Gochel dwyllo dy fargeinwyr,
Duw sydd Farnwr ar y twyllwyr;
Pe dihengit tu hwnt i'r Werddon
Duw fyn ddial twyll y porthmon.

Byth ni rostia un o'r twyllwyr,
'Rhyn a heliant, medd y 'Sgrythur;
Ni ddaw twyll i neb yn ennill,
Fe red ymaith fel trwy ridyll.

Gochel feddwi wrth borthmona,
Gwin hel borthmon i gardota,
Os y porthmon a fydd meddw,
Fe a'r holl stoc i brynu cwrw.

Dela'n union, carca d'enaid;
Na ddiflanna â da gwirioniaid;
Pe diflannit i'r Low Cwntres,
Dial Duw a fyn d'orddiwes.

Rhys Prichard,
Cannwyll y Cymry (arg. 1807), Caerfyrddin 1907, tt. 148-149

Advice to Drovers, by Vicar Prichard (1549-1644)

If you are a drover, deal honestly,
Pay a fair price for what you get;
Keep your word, do not break promises;
Better than gold in a purse is credit;

Do not try to take advantage of the poor,
Do not greed for over profit;
Do not huckster with arch thieves,
Nothing of theirs is of value.

Beware of buying much on credit,
Do not take people at their word;
Buying on credit makes a drover
Leave the country and flee to Ireland.

Beware of cheating on your bargainer,
God will judge you for deceiving.
If you flee beyond to Ireland
God will avenge a dealer's cheating.

Do not shield the ones that cheat
All they collect, so say the Scrptures;
Cheating will not turn to gain
But will vanish through a sieve.

Do not get drunk while you are droving,
Wine will drive a drover to begging,
If the drover is a drunkard,
All his stock will buy his beer.

Deal honestly and save your soul;
Do not steal goods from the simple;
Even if you hide in the Low Centres,
God's revenge will overpower you.

Rhys Prichard,
Cannwyll y Cymry (1807 ed.), Carmarthen 1907, pp. 148-149

Appendix 4

The Agreement of Sale for a Fulham business betwen
Edward Evans and Llewelyn and Anne Evans in 1936.
(Mary Bott)

Appendix 5

The Agreement of Sale for a Rotherlithe business between
Rees Edwards and Daniel Lloyd.

(John Lloyd)

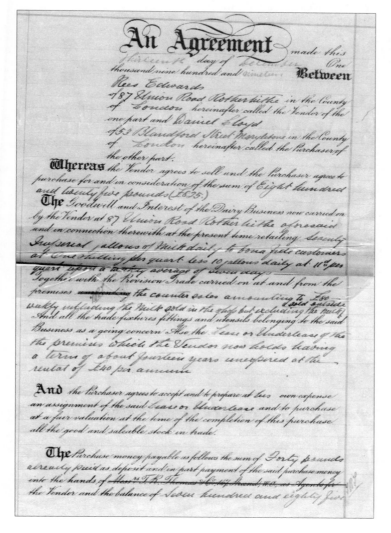

Appendix 6

Statement of Settlement between John Morgan Williams and Messrs Morgans for the Dairy at 38 Hartington Road, South Lambeth in January 1921. The agent arranging the contract was a Welshman.

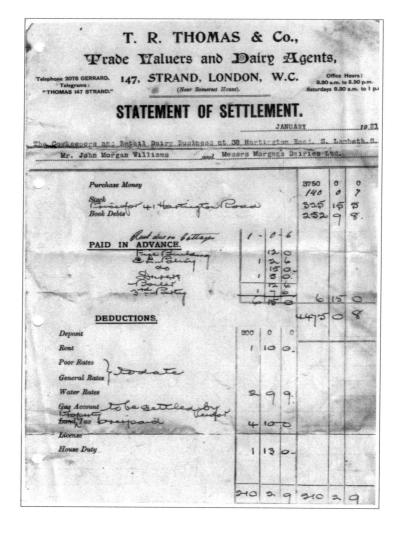

Appendix 7

Statement of Settlement between E Roscoe Lloyd (vendor)
a Mrs E Nicholas (purchaser) for the Dairy at 215 Acton
Lane, Chiswick in 1933. The agent was again a Welshman.

PHONE : Office   Gerrard 1430.
       Private   Park 7117.

W. T H O M A S,

Dairy Agent,

4 3, O X F O R D S T R E E T, W. 1.
Opposite Frascati's. Nr. Tottenham Crt Rd. Tube.

STATEMENT OF SETTLEMENT.

18th   December,   1933.

Business at 215, Acton Lane, Chiswick, London, W.3., by Mr. E. R. Lloyd.

Purchased by Mrs. E. Nicholas, 94, High Street, Hornsey. N. 8.

				£	s	d
Purchase Money				1925	0	0
Stock				69	4	4
Book Debts				44	10	1
Paid in Advance by Vendor :						
Fire Insurance & Plate Glass Insurance paid to Sept. 29th 1934 @ £2-5-0 p.a. - 287 days.		1	15	4		
General Rates Paid to 31st March, 1934 - 105 days		7	2	2		
Insurance. Fire of Workmen Compensation etc						
Third Party, £1. Burning Risk 10/8 all Paid to 25th March 1934. - 99 days			15	8		
				9	13	2
				2048	7	7
DEDUCTIONS :						
Deposit	100	0	0			
Rent due from 25th Nov., to 16th Dec 1933. -21 dys	4	1	8			
General Rates due from 30th Sept to 16th Dec.	5	4	3			
Water Rates due from 30th Sept. to 16th Dec.		15	3			
Gas Account ... ... Settled by Vendor.						
Electric Light Account						
Property Tax						
				104	16	11
			£	1943	10	8

Appendix 8
More on the Milk Trail

Mary Bott and her mother outside their Fulham shop
(Mary Bott)

In the family shop in Fulham
(Mary Bott)

The Evans Brothers milk cart, Hampstead
(Rod Davies)

Parry-Williams family shop in Replingham Road, Southfield
(John and Jennie Parry Williams)

Sultan Stores: Leisa Jones and colleague outside their shop in Sultan Street
(Edwin Jones)

T. D. Davies' shop (Dilys Scott)

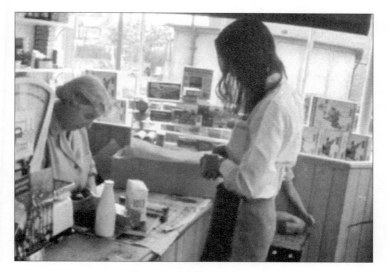

Rhys Jones' Lilse Street shop
(Evan Jones, Bethania)

A Hampshire Street dairy milk cart in the mid 50s
(Richard and Jois Snelson)

Acknowledgements

This book would not have seen the light of day had it not been for the people listed here – people who gave of their time, who invited me into their homes, visited me, communicated by letter, e-mail and phone, who loaned me photographs to scan and generally convinced me that it was a project that needed doing. My grateful thanks to all. I sincerely apologise for any inadverdent omissions.

Peggy Beaven, London
Mary Bott, Aberporth
Christine Boudier, London
Carys Bidden, Taliesin
Eileen Brigshaw, Aber-arth
Anna Bruton, LW Family History Society

Olive Corner, Porthcawl

Alun Eirug Davies, Aberystwyth
Betty Davies, Aber-porth
Eilir Ann Daniels, Cricieth
Eleri Davies, Aberystwyth
Elgan Davies, Newcastle Emlyn
G. Davies, Brentwood
Emrys Davies, Brynaman
Gareth Davies, Ealing Green
John Davies, Llanrhystud
Nest Mary Daniels (nee Lewis), Llandeilo
Rod and Rosie Davies, Llanfihangel-ar-arth
Roger Davies, Llanwrtyd
Russell Davies
Teifi Davies, Sarnau

Anne Edwards, Watford
Elizabeth Evans
Evan and Carol Evans, Tal-y-bont
Goronwy Evans, Lampeter
Gwyn Evans
Ifor Evans, Machynlleth
Jane Evans
Megan Evans, Dulwich
Rhiannon Evans, Tregaron

Cledwyn Fychan, Llanddeiniol

Mair Griffiths, Llanddewibrefi
Betty Griffiths, Aberystwyth
Blodwen Griffiths, Abergwili
Rhidian Griffiths, Aberystwyth
Heather Grosse (hegrose@waitrose.com)

Siw Hartson, Capel Seion/ Ealing Green
Richard and Bethan Hartnup, Bow Street
Emyr Hopkins, Tregaron
Margaret Humphreys, Machynlleth

Andrew James, Llandysul
Mair James, Llangeitho
Gwenllian Jenkins, Llanfabon, Caerffili
Kitty Jenkins, Lledrod
Aled Jones, Cilcennin
Andrew and Pat Jones, Cwm-ann
Aneurin Jones, Lampeter
Ann Jones, Bronnant
Edwin Jones, Cross Inn
Eluned Jones, Pinner
Emrys Jones, Aberaeron

Evan Jones, Cardiff
Evan Jones, Bethania
Evan Jones, Llanddewibrefi
Helen Jones, Aberaeron
Henry Jones, London
Iwan Jones, Lampeter
John Richards-Jones, Llanwrtyd
Jon Meirion Jones, Llangrannog
Lloyd Jones, Talgarreg
Mary L. Jones, Brynaman
Oriel Jones, Llanfihangel-ar-arth

Emrys Lewis, Brynaman
Euros Lewis, Cribyn
Iris Lewis, Llanrhystud
Jennie Lewis, Barnet
John Lewis, Aberaeron
John Lewis, London
Rees Glyn Lewis, Colwyn Bay
Evana Lloyd, Aberaeron
Huw Lloyd, Abergele
Ifor and Myfanwy Lloyd, Pennant
John Lloyd, Aberystwyth
Lewis Lloyd, London
Trefor Lloyd-Jones, Amersham

Gwen Manley, Talybont
Audrey Morgan, Aberaeron
Dai Morgan, Borth
Evan Morgan, Cardiff
Gareth and Geraint Morgan, London
Tom and Bethan Morgan, Aberaeron
Trefor and Mair Morgan, Aberystwyth

Anne Owen

Ieuan Parry, Blaenplwyf
Janet Parry Jones, Cardiff
John and Jennie Parry-Williams, Blaenplwyf
Gwyn Pickering, London
Jo Pleshakov, Vancouver
Maldwyn Pugh, Amersham

Dilys Scott, Weymouth
Margaret Sharp, Aberystwyth
Richard and Jois Snelson, Denbigh

Ann Thomas, Watford
Annabelle Thomas, Llanwrtyd
Elizabeth Thomas, London
Hazel Thomas, Aberysywth
Hywel and Elinor Thomas, London
Margaret Thomas, Aber-arth

David and Margaret Wells, Ontario
Bowen Williams, New Barnet
Jeannette Williams
Nigel Williams, London

A special thank you to Margaret Williams, Wembley for suggesting many useful connections.

I am indebted to the following Institutions:
The British Library
Ceredigion Archives
Ceredigion Library (Aberaeron Branch)
Kensington Central Library
The KitKat Restaurant, Toronto

The London Welsh Family History Society
The National Library of Wales
The Talbot Hotel, Tregaron

A sincere thank you to Lyn Ebenezer for his endless patience and enthusiasm without which this project would have died an early death. Thank you also to Nia Roberts from Gwasg Garreg Gwalch who read the Welsh script and made many useful suggestions, particularly suggesting that I enlarge the meaning of 'goodwill' as it applied to the purchase of a business.

Aneurin Jones's help with the translation is especially appreciated.

And a big thank you to Lyn Ebenezer for his translations of the Drover verses.

Principal Sources

Aberdare Leader 22 January 1870

Aberystwyth Observer 9 June 1904

Atkins, P.J.: London's intra-urban milk supply circa 1790-1914, published 1977. *Transactions of the Institute of British Geographers.* New Series 2

Barcud, Y, Rhifyn 7 1976: Hanes Porthmon gan Mrs. Jane Davies

Booth, Charles: The Life and Labour of the Poor in London 1896-1903. Report

Bowen, E.G. Various documents in the National Library and personal conversations with Richard J. Colyer

Carmarthenshire Historian. Some References to the Cattle Drovers and Carmarthen. Volume 1 1961

Colyer, Richard J.: Welsh Cattle Drovers in the Nineteenth Century. *National Library of Wales Journal* Winter 1972 XVII/4 (1), Summer 1974 XVIII/3 (2) and Summer 1975 XIX (3)

Colyer, Richard J.: *The Welsh Cattle Drovers.* University of Wales Press, Cardiff

County Observer and Monmouth Central Adviser 4 March 1876

Dickens, Charles: *Oliver Twist.* John Williams 1838

Ellis, T. I.: *Crwydro Llundain.* Christopher Davies Gwasg Merlin 1971

Emmanuel, Alun

Evans, Daniel (Daniel Ddu o Geredigion): *Gwinllan y Bardd* 1831

Evans, Idris: *Hard Road to London.* Steptoes 2009

Farmers Magazine 1856

Francis-Jones, Gwyneth: *Cows, Cardis and Cockneys.* Camelot, Y Borth 1984

Gloucester Journal 4 August 1897

Hughes, Marjorie: *Atgofion Llanfihangel-y-creuddyn a Llundain*. Garn Chapel, Rhyd-y-pennau website
Jenkins, Dan: *Cerddi Ysgol Llanycrwys*. Gwasg Gomer 1934
Jenkins, R.T.: *Hanes Cymru yn y Ddeunawfed Ganrif*. Gwasg Prifysgol Cymru, Caerdydd 1928
R. T. Jenkins: *Y Ffordd yng Nghymru*. Hughes a'i Fab 1933
Jones, Emrys (ed): *The Welsh in London 1500-2000*. Cymmrodorion 2001
Jones, Evann: *Cerdded Hen Ffeiriau*. Cymdeithas Lyfrau Ceredigion 1972
Jones, Jon M.: *Morwyr y Cilie*. Cyhoeddiadau Barddas 2002
Leech, Alan: *Dan Jenkins Pentrefelin*. Y Lolfa 2011
Prichard, Rhys: *Cannwyll y Cymry*. Carmarthen 1807
Rhys, Manon: *Siglo'r Crud*, 1998; *Rhannu'r Gwely*, 1999; *Cwilt Rhacs*, 1999. Gomer (Trioled y Palmant Aur).
Roberts, Glyn: *I Take This City*. Jarrods 1933
Roberts, Gomer M.: *Y Ddinas Gadarn: Hanes Eglwys Jewin*. Pwyllgor Dathlu Daucanmlwyddiant Eglwys Jewin 1974
Roberts, Gomer M.: *Dafydd Jones o Gaeo*. Gwasg Aberystwyth 1948
The Star 1937
Taylor, David: *London's Milk Supply 1850-1900*. Agricultural History Society 1971
Thomas, Dylan: *Under Milk Wood*. J.M. Dent 1958
Welsh Gazette February 1928
Welsh National Bazaar in Aid of the London C.M. Churches. Report 1912.
Wentham, E.H.: *The London Welsh Milk Trade 1860-1900*. Economic History Review. New Series 1964
Williams, Llewelyn (ed): *Hanes Eglwys y Tabernacl Kings Cross 1847-1947*. Llundain 1947
Williams-Davies, John: *Merched y Gerddi: A Seasonal Migration of Female Labour from Rural Wales*. Folk Life No. 15, 1977